AIPF Annual Workshop Series 1

Socialism in the 21st Century

Edited by

Anil Rajimwale

M. Vijaya Kumar

AAKAR

All India Progressive Forum (AIPF)

President

Prof. K.S. Chalam (M) 077022 00026
chalamks@hotmail.com

Working President

M. Vijaya Kumar (M) 098489 33545
marlavk@yahoo.com

General Secretary

Anil Rajimwale (M) 098685 25812
anilrajim@gmail.com

Proceedings of All India Symposium
January 28-30, 2008, Hyderabad organised by NRRR Centre and AIPF

First Published 2018

ISBN 978-93-5002-514-7

Published by
AAKAR BOOKS
28 E Pocket IV, Mayur Vihar Phase I, Delhi 110 091
Phones : 011 2279 5505, 2279 5641
aakarbooks@gmail.com; www.aakarbooks.com

In Association with
Neelam Rajasekhara Reddy Research Centre for Social Sciences, Kondapur, (Via) Gachibowli
Chandra Rajeshwara Rao Marg, Hyderabad 502 084
and
All India Progressive Forum, New Delhi

Designed by
Limited Colors, Delhi 110 092

Printed at
Sapra Brothers, Delhi 110 092

Contents

Foreword

Socialism of the 21st century is not a futuristic dream. We are already in the 21st century. It is imperative that we make our ideas clear about what kind of a socialist society we wish to build, and we should do it fast—for the simple reason that new ideas are needed to deal with today's rapidly changing world.

At the dawn of this millennium, there is a new hope about the future of Marxism-Leninism. Extensive work is going on around the world, with Communist and Workers' Parties in many countries searching for concretizing their ideas about socialism in the 21st century, with each country's national pecularities.

The Neelam Rajasekhara Reddy Research Centre for Social Sciences, Hyderabad has organised an All-India Symposium from January 28–30, 2008 on "Socialism in the 21st Century" at Hyderabad. The participants in the three-day symposium are specialists in Marxist studies from all over the country. The historical background of building socialism in the last century as well as the philosophical, economic and sociological aspects of building socialism in the coming days were deliberated in the symposium. Also deliberated were topics on Marxism and modern science, socialism and democracy and a host of other topics. The symposium is the culmination of nearly a year's efforts by our Research Institute. I greatly appreciate the efforts of the organisers in successfully conducting the symposium and for arranging this collection of papers presented at the symposium in the form of a book.

Y.V. Krishna Rao

Introduction

It was a symposium organised in the wake of the worldwide debates on the collapse of the Soviet Union and the East European regimes. It began as a series of annual symposiums/seminars/workshops organised by AIPF till today. At that time, in 2008, the AIPF was not yet formally involved, though the organisers were more or less those associated with it. Later, the workshops began to be organised by and in the name of AIPF, sometimes in association with the NRRR Centre.

The first symposium was organised by the NRRR Centre (Neelam Rajsekhar Reddy Research Centre), Hyderabad. The collapse of socialism-oriented regimes in the Soviet Union and Eastern Europe raised several debatable issues of aspects of theory and practice of socialism. Many favoured a re-assessment of the history of the revolution. Many others observed that the issue was related to the STR and the new era inaugurated with it.

The collapse and related questions have opened up a fruitful debate on a host of questions. It was felt that they must be discussed in detail. It was also felt that many old instruments of knowledge and formulations were outdated.

The organisers decided to hold discussions on as many aspects as possible. Therefore, papers and sessions cover wide areas like: nature and impact of STR, socialism of the future, democracy and socialism, a critical re-evaluation of socialism in the 20th century, gender issue, interpretation of globalization and neoliberalism, meaning of socialism in the 21st century, importance of democratic revolution and institutions, etc.

Hon. Director of NRRR Centre (late) Y.V. Krishna Rao, Director of the Centre Raghavachary, M. Vijaya Kumar as the Symposium Organiser, and others played an important role in the symposium.

We hope, the papers and proceedings will help to clarify many issues.

Comments and criticism are welcome.

Anil Rajimwale
Coordinator of the Symposium

1

Socialism in the 21st Century

The Basic Questions

Anil Rajimwale

We live in an era of the greatest and most rapid changes and transformations, as never before in the history of mankind. The transformations are caused by the Scientific and Technological Revolution (STR) and its consequence, the Information and Communication Revolution (ICR). They are changing the context, dimensions and meanings of socialism, which need to be worked out.

It is an era of internationalisation and integration, in which these changes are distorted and misinterpreted by certain imperialist circles as globalisation, which is sought to be tagged along with privatisation and liberalisation. While older types of socialist regimes have collapsed in the erstwhile USSR and Eastern Europe, events in Latin America and elsewhere express an endeavour to reformulate the democratic process. It may help us to trace the future paths to socialist transformations.

In this era, the working people of the whole world can together fight neo-imperialism, and can solve many crucial problems of humanity. STR and ICR provide new ways, means and weapons to fight for the solution of the problems. At the same time many new problems have arisen, which concern the whole of humanity, and just this or that class, such as environmental pollution and the ecological crisis. They can only be dealt with through joint efforts on a world scale. Hence too the significance of integration and internationalisation. We should not fall a prey to the false consciousness being created under the garb of globalisation.

There are several potentials for the future in the present.

All the structures and constituent parts of world society: state, civil society, classes, relations of socio-economic and political-ideological nature are being redefined. Importance of democracy has enhanced as never before. New strata are coming into being; classes and their boundaries are being redefined; the social composition of the society at the world level and in our country is changing, setting new tasks and methods of approach for the transformative and revolutionary forces. Class struggles are assuming new forms, new areas and sections of struggle besides class struggle are coming up, e.g. castes, strata, holistic human values, culture, environment, etc. A rapidly integrating world market is emerging. Unprecedented changes are in the offing.

Scientific and Technological Revolution (STR)

STR is the single most important and decisive factor of the present-day world changes. The Industrial Revolution of the past began an industrial age, which continues till today. It brought in its wake qualitative changes in the nature of production, created industrial and capitalist societies. It was also an era of emergence of Marxism and other transformative theories. Huge socialist experiments, both partially successful and unsuccessful, were carried on in this age. It was and is a practically and theoretically rich era. Much is to be learnt from socialism and revolutions: both failed and successful.

STR is basically a radical change in the means of production, as also in communication and information, based on the use of microchips, electronics, computers, satellites, and now mobile technology. It needs to be studied in depth for its implications and potentials—both technological and social. Beginning in the 1950s (transistors), the STR gathered speed through the 1960s, 70s, 80s and 90s to the present century.

Today, STR has created a cover of consciousness around the earth in form of internet and e-mail based upon computer networks, satellite transmission, websites, etc. The STR is now proceeding into the next stage with nano technologies and the impending superconductivity revolution.

The STR and ICR have drastically changed the concepts of time and space in daily life practice, in addition to their theoretical workout. Information and knowledge travel, today, instantly, crossing the various traditional barriers. This is a novel way to form global and local consciousness.

Changing Social Composition

The STR and ICR are causing widespread and deep changes in the social composition, presenting new problems before the sociopolitical movements and their strategies. New sections of working people, engineers, programmers, middle class employees, call-centre young workers, information/knowledge workers, and so on are crystallising. Many older sections of the society are going into the background or are disappearing.

Major changes in the working class composition are taking place. It is no more the working class of Marx's time: proletariat and "nothing to lose but its chains". Vast sections have much to lose. The periphery and boundaries of this class are expanding rapidly, so much so that it has caused a debate as to the nature of today's working class. Some people would like to call it 'working people' rather than working class.

Knowledge workers constitute a growingly important segment of the working class. The composition of the class is changing from this point of view too: in favour of information/knowledge and away from production workers. It is a change/shift in terms of nature and relative proportions (knowledge, production), and not necessarily in terms of numbers.

These changes call for a change in approach to the new workers.

A new middle 'class' comprising a vast strata of intermediate sections is emerging. They constitute a growing section of society, with contradictory tendencies. They play an important role in society, and this role is growing. They are conveyors of information, ideas, policies, cultural/social attitudes and values, and set examples, both positive and negative, for the rest of the society.

With the growth and concentration of urban centres, and an intensification of the process of urbanisation, the middle strata play a greater role. Mass work and radicalisation of these sections assume growing importance.

Vast new sections of small-scale and medium-scale entrepreneurs, businessmen, and people attached to them are coming up. The STR is rendering the means of production and information smaller in scale. This, along with many other factors, has made possible the emergence of individual and small-scale proprietors. This point is usually ignored. The tendency of production (enterprises, factories, units, etc.) to grow larger has largely (not entirely) been reversed (large units can still be found, and continue to be built, though). Now the tendency of production is towards smaller scales.

This is why, we find larger numbers of small entrepreneurs, as new modern and more assertive sections, pressing for a proper place in the market and productive competition. Workshop owners, lathe operator-cum-owners, computer owners-operators, etc. participate in a big way in socio-economic activities. Information and image operators/ creators are increasingly acquiring greater importance.

The modern entrepreneurial and capitalist class is being revamped, particularly the vast sections of petty, small and medium producers and businessmen, who, for their own interest, try to come out of various shackles. This class today is becoming more multilayered and complex.

The STR/ICR and the emergence of the globalised market has, at the same time, enabled big and finance capital to grow rapidly in operations, and become more independent of production. Relatively independent finance capital is making the rounds of the earth, seeking super-profits, trying to strangle smaller capitals, entrepreneurs and common people, and trying to establish its sway over the world.

While independent small businesses emerge fast, finance capital tries to throw them out of the stage altogether. From time to time, finance capital touches the productive sphere, but generally it need not.

Modern finance capital is the most ominous development of the present times.

MNCs have reached unprecedented new levels, assuming new forms and structures. Farmers, small business and mass of people have to confront them and other giant businesses. At the same time, modern big business and MNCs are also depositories of much of the new technology.

At the same time, giant monopolies and finance capital are not able to have their way all the time. Medium and small scale production and business, and local capital is also becoming stronger because of many factors, one being the STR and the consequent tendency towards smaller scales of the means of production. These sections of entrepreneurs and capitalist class are challenging the big business on a world scale. They are giving them a tough fight in the world market. Export of the Indian, Chinese and other goods on larger scales, and the panic they create among the giant monopolies and imperialists, are examples. Within the WTO, the developing countries are increasingly grouping and regrouping themselves to present a joint front to the imperialist countries, in particular the US.

The role and activities of small and medium-scale capital are also increasing. Possibilities of shifting the capitalist direction in the non-monopoly, democratic capitalist direction has increased.

Changing Nature of Work and Production

On a much deeper and theoretical level, the STR and the ICR are causing a change in the nature of work and production process. Marx, in his famous work *Grundrisse*, has analysed the separation of the work process from the production process as a result of large-scale automation. It was his genius to have seen that in full or near-full automation, the worker and work are separated out of the production process, and the worker becomes an *observer of the production process*. He has to do no more than switch on the system and allow it to operate on its own.

This observation becomes more relevant in the context of today's technological revolution, whereby the means of production and communication are being automated owing to the application of electronics. This question needs greater analyses and treatment.

These changes also bring to the fore the question of changes in the nature of ownership under socialism/communism.

Marxism: The Frontier Thinking

Marxism is the most influential and advanced thought-system today. No other theory has left such a deep and long-lasting impact on history, as Marxism has.

Marx effected a qualitative leap in theory and practice by his great discoveries and seminal works. He studied and synthesised all the great philosophies, schools of thought and discoveries of natural and social sciences into a new, higher system. His achievements are yet to be surpassed. He synthesised philosophies into higher levels of dialectical materialism, materialist conception of history and integrated relationships of matter and consciousness. He made great and lasting discoveries into modes of production, particularly the capitalist mode of production, e.g. that of surplus value. He, along with Engels, studied everything new and latest in his times, both in natural sciences (see, *Dialectics of Nature*), and social and economic sciences (e.g. Capital, etc.). Lenin made his own contributions, carrying forward their work. His *Materialism and Empirio-criticism* in philosophy, and *Two Tactics* stand out in the wide field of theoretical investigations. Lenin continued the work of Marx further, and was a thinker of the same calibre and incisiveness as the latter. He was also the leader of the first successful revolution.

Marxism is a frontier science, philosophy and thought system because Marx grasped everything that was new, novel and emerging in the material world, society and thought of his times. It was his great theoretical work and discoveries that put the social movement for emancipation, particularly the working class movement, on a new basis with a clear-cut world view. The world was to change forever after that.

Marxism inspired many revolutions and socialist experiments the world over. They are useful both in their successes, failures and inadequacies. Various interpretations of Marxist theories in this or that field have been put forward by their rulers of the socialist countries and by other interpreters. There has been much debate and polemics over 'state bureaucratic socialism', particularly between 'Western Marxism' and official and orthodox Marxism. It has been opined by Louis Althusser and others that the ruling parties of the Socialist countries were driven more by their ideological and other interests than by people's interests. Consequently, the state became a distorted 'ideological' one, violating the spirit and letter of Marxism.

Many outstanding Marxists had been warning and criticising the existing socialism and its theory and practice. Among them Maxim Gorky, Rosa Luxemburg, Bukharin, Lukacs, Gramsci, Italian, Spanish, French and many other communists and Marxists.

Rosa Luxemburg criticised (*Russian Revolution and Leninism or Marxism*) the style of functioning of the Russian Communist Party and the Soviets, and warned of usurpation of power by a clique in the name of the working class. She criticised Lenin himself.

In her opinion and in the opinion of many others, power passed from the Soviets to the Party, from the Party to the central committee, then to the politburo, and to the coterie of a handful, thus preparing the way for one-party, even one person rule.

So, the question of real exercise of power by the working class under socialism still remains an unresolved practical and theoretical problem.

The question of existing socialism (including the ones that collapsed) needs to be examined in depth. The problem of the relationship between democracy and socialism remains unresolved till today. No satisfactory socialist model of democracy exists. The existing regimes, despite their great achievements in many fields, remain one-party rule, with no freedom for dissent.

Antonio Gramsci tried to come to terms with many questions of democracy and cultural freedom.

On the question of democracy and socialism, the phenomenon of Stalinism and Maoism within the Communist parties and in the socialist countries, has been studied and criticised. Stalinism arose much before the war and continued long afterwards and continues to exist. War conditions have sometimes been presented as justification for Stalinist repressions, whose main victims were the communists themselves. But it arose much earlier and in quite different contexts. Both Lenin and Luxemburg had warned against it. Stalinism and Maoism arose as a system, and not as just individual aberrations; they sought to justify violation of democracy in the party and the society on the pretext of certain economic and political difficulties. They evolved into a system, with high concentration of all kinds of power in the hands of one or few. This question needs deeper and more serious examination.

The centralised bureaucratic socialist system was incongruous for its times both before and after the Second World War. In today's context of worldwide democratic transformations and STR/ICR, it is totally out of place.

Today, Marxism faces fresh challenges and tasks. These challenges become highlighted in the context of imperialist offensive, which seeks to deny the importance of Marxism since Marx himself, on the pretext of failure of the centralised bureaucratic socialist regimes.

The challenges go far beyond this framework. The post-Second World War development caused many amendments and changes in Marxist concepts. Some were given up, e.g. dictatorship of the proletariat. Others are being debated, even questioned, such as the classical Leninist theory of imperialism, general crisis of world capitalism, nature of the working class, multi-party system in socialism, role of culture and ideas in the socialist system, which was underestimated, role and place of religion, freedom for press and organisation and parties in socialism, etc.

By the way, it was CPI, which recognised through its Constitution adopted in 1958, the existence of the multi-party system with provision even for opposition parties in the future socialism.

Changes in Latin America and Other Places

Installation of Left-leaning and democratic presidents and regimes in eight countries of Latin America has underlined the great role, in the present times, of democratic and revolutionary change of governments through parliamentary institutions, backed by mass support, given the neutrality of the armed forces. There are many lessons for the future in the events in Latin America.

Most importantly, the social composition of Latin America has undergone a change. New working middle class sections, new young workers, increasing role of young women and housewives, students and youth, new farmers, together with older sections/ classes, rising entrepreneurs, democratic sections of the capitalist class and bourgeoisie, have entered the active arena of democratic transformation, with the struggle against US imperialism as the main reference point. Various Left, Marxist, workers' parties, democratic and progressive parties and organisations play the main role together and separately. A broad social and political coalition has come up on the scale of society.

The democratic advance in Latin America needs to be studied deeply for its implications for the state, democracy, socialism, market, reforms, press, new strata, role of civil society, nature and forms of revolutions and ideologies. In a wider sense, the same applies to the rest of the world, particularly Western Europe, Italy, Nepal, changes in Eastern Europe, Asia, and of course India.

We are undoubtedly passing through a great transition.

Theory of Marxism

Rapid changes in the post-Second World War period necessitate suitable updating of Marxism. Otherwise, there is every danger of its falling behind the times. Marx and Lenin kept abreast and ahead of the times: from natural sciences to social sciences—a wide horizon of deep and frontier theories.

Today, the transformations are rapid as never before. Innumerable questions regarding the present and the future are being thrown up. We have to identify the dialectics of the emergence of the new and the latest. Only then can we determine future directions. And only then can Marxism become livelier and develop as a frontier theory. While we identify what is relevant and forceful in Marxism, we should also identify what is not so relevant or not relevant at all, and add new dimensions to theory. Relationships of caste, class, community and culture in our country, the increasing role of parliamentary institutions, backed by mass activity, giant strides of mass media as the fourth estate, role of women and youth, environment, culture, language, quantum revolution, changes in the nature of the means of production and communication are some points to ponder. How different will be the future socialism/ communism from the past concepts and practice is very important. Parliamentary institutions down to the village have come to stay. It is possible to create Left-backed or Leftist governments in various parts of the world. People are already talking of "a new world is possible".

It is an ambitious task to identify transformations the world over. The world is fast integrating, unified markets, political entities and communication systems are coming up, the nature of the state, the classes, democracy, media is changing, prolonged democratic transformations as a process with step by step shifts in balance of forces, cross-class questions like environment, global market, information/knowledge flows, etc. are some of the relevant questions.

Regional integration in Europe, Latin America and elsewhere need to be analysed, not just for their negative aspects, emphasised by imperialism and MNCs, but also for the positive and objective aspects, particularly for their relevance for the theory of state and market integration, and for their great potentials. Dialectics of the national and international are in operation.

Role of Market

Market is an inalienable part of society. National and international markets are sought to be dominated by US imperialism and the giant MNCs. At the same time, common people, ordinary producers and consumers, entrepreneurs, peasants, working people, etc. need greater space and say in market. Hence the need for democratic shifts in the national and world market. It is necessary to give up a totally negative attitude to the market and reforms.

Need for New Concepts

New concepts are emerging in philosophy, economics, political theory, natural sciences, etc. They need to be studied in detail. Other theoretical schools need to be analysed and researched in depth. Among them are post-modernism, post-industrialism, post-structuralism and other 'post' theories; existentialism, 'Western' Marxism, many underground works created in the former Soviet Union and countries of east Europe (see, for example, Roy Medvedev, etc.), China's experiences, etc.

The Frankfurt and Copenhagen Schools contributed a great deal to the development of critical theory. Marxism needs to interact in these fields.

Marxism followed a certain sense of security in the conditions of existing socialism. As a result, certain orthodox, 'official' and rigid concepts were followed as fixed concepts. As a result, the role of ideas, culture, linguistic philosophy, social institutions developing in the civil society (see Antonio Gramsci), mass media, environmental degradation, market forces, greater role of small-scale production, feminism, urbanisation, and so on and so forth, were paid inadequate attention.

Consequently, other theoretical and ideological trends have sought to fill the gap, of course, in their own way. They have many positive aspects/concepts, which should be assimilated, the negative ones criticised and rejected.

Some of the tasks before Marxism may be identified; of course that does not exhaust the 'list':

- Assimilate the discoveries and general concepts of new levels of science and technology.
- Draw relevant concepts from the STR/ICR. Now we are going over to nano-technology and mobile communications.
- Assimilate the findings of genetics and genetic engineering, biotechnology, new biology, etc.
- It has become essential to look deeply at electronics and computer revolution, Internet technology, etc. and their role in the formation of our consciousness.
- It has become absolutely essential to study and assimilate the concepts of relativity (special and

general), quantum mechanics, quantum philosophy, changing concepts of space and time, material and direct bases of idea, concept of 'reality' (cf. virtual reality), brain—computer interface, etc.

Marxist philosophy needs to be enriched with quantum philosophy and relativity, a task left largely unattended.

- We need to evolve from the Newtonian world-view into Einsteinian relativistic/quantum one and even beyond.
- Role of language, idea, subject and subject—object relationship, etc. linguistic philosophy presents many novel ideas, as also post-modernism (at the same time they present several conservative notions).
- Study and assimilation of the nature and role of the modern state, classes, parties, civil society, etc.
- Civil society, social institutions and culture should find more active space in Marxism.
- An analysis of present-day imperialism and finance capital. Its study by Marxism is inadequate; it is more subjective than objective. Their structure, institutions, etc. need to be gone into. The US imperialist system is becoming tangible and a concrete opponent of and hurdle for the whole world.
- Lenin says we cannot become 'real Marxists' without studying Hegel. Today, in the world of rapid changes, study and application of dialectics has become more important. There is a revived interest in Hegel's dialectics. Dialectics needs to be developed further in the present context. Quantum mechanics and quantum philosophy create favourable grounds for development of dialectics as never before.
- Shifts in the capitalist mode of production towards information, knowledge, services.

Information/communication is becoming a bigger sector than production.

- Nature of operation of law of value and of labour theory of value in modem industry and services.
- Study Chinese experiences. Also other countries ruled by the CPs.
- New features of Indian revolution, etc.

Role of Knowledge/Information

There can be no two opinions that knowledge and information are playing an increasingly important role in contemporary world. Some theorists even talk of a 'knowledge society' for a not so remote future. We can talk of a 'socialist knowledge society' in the same vein.

With the spectrum of society shifting rapidly towards information, and away from production, one may ponder over the concept of 'mode of information' (as Mark Poster, 1993, does in the vein of mode of production, though he has his own interpretations). With knowledge and information becoming, step by step, the most influential factors, it would be fruitful to enquire into the future society based upon knowledge. Production then would become acutely effective, yet rapidly constricted.

This also contains germs of a social order oriented towards better distribution, productivity having reached very high levels. Means of production today are changing fast and are reaching new levels of maturity, becoming extremely productive. Material conditions for the solution of basic problems of society appear to be emerging. Solutions to the mode of distribution in the new contexts have to be found. Mature productive and communicative forces create favourable material conditions for socialism and communism.

Another very important question to be dealt with is the transition of socialism/communism to the postindustrial stage and to the new levels of productive forces. The theory of postindustrialism may be discussed and debated. That is another matter. The question is that the technological revolution is changing the nature and direction of the tools, machines and equipment. It is no more developing towards the larger scales, but towards the smaller scales. Therefore, the question of development beyond the industrial nature and management of production and communication becomes relevant. It may be worthwhile to enquire as to what will be the nature of socialism and communism in the postindustrial era and organisation of things. Can socialism make such a transition, and how?

In such a situation, what will the nature of ownership be under socialism and communism? Obviously, one cannot rule out individual ownership, particularly today and in future. Marx himself did not entirely rule this out. This point needs consideration. Discourse, dialogue and discussion should become a common way of life in the conditions of ICR.

Changing Structure and Composition of Society

Very soon, a majority, more than half of the population of the world will be living in urban areas. This applies to India as well. Urbanisation is accelerating.

Agrarian population in Western Europe, Japan and the US is already below ten per cent, and their proportion is still falling. There is a rapid shift in the structure and composition of population towards those in services, exchange, and information/knowledge. A vast middle and working section is appearing. Giant urban conglomerates, mega-cities and metropolises are emerging.

These changes are of great significance for the future of revolutionary and democratic forces. How do we create movement and impart consciousness to the new urban centres? A large section of people is unconnected with past history. Traditional bases of the movement (e.g. various industries like textiles, etc.) are disappearing. Workers in the new sectors are still to establish contacts with the movement.

Urban residential areas present potential bases for the movement, but they are yet to be tapped. The Left, democratic and revolutionary movements have still to establish strong bases among these areas and sections. This is true of India as well as many other countries of the world. To oppose the existing system, to accelerate democratisation of society, free from imperialist domination, in and through these highly concentrated centres, is a major challenge. Thus, several new paths of revolutionary transformations may evolve. The main movement today has to be in the urban areas.

Marxism and Battle of Ideas

Marxism can proceed further in the battle of ideas only as frontier thinking in the conditions of ICR by mastering dialectics fully. It has to assimilate everything new: from quantum world to market to production, changing nature of work and labour process, etc. We can update Marxist dialectics and philosophy by adding new aspects and notions from various fields of reality and theory.

Marxism and Natural Sciences

Unprecedented new developments are taking place and concepts emerging in the vast field of natural sciences: genetics, biotechnology, quantum mechanics, human-computer and brain-computer interfaces, nanotechnology, space-time relationship, relativity and many other fields. The practical, philosophical and conceptual conclusions being reached by these sciences need to be synthesised in the form of higher levels of theoretical praxis.

Marxism and Environment

The question of environment has today become a crucial one for the very existence of human species and for life itself. It involves conceptualisation at holistic levels of human society. It is one of those emerging realities that transcend the entire planet and, therefore, need a higher level of abstraction. Crisis of environment forces us to rethink our strategies of development and to re-create the relationship between nature and development. This task cannot be ignored, as the events of global warming and ecological degradation warn us.

Thus human thought, in particular Marxism, stands on the verge of a giant leap.

Socialism of the 21st Century

How different would the 21st century socialism be? What are the new challenges before it? What will be the nature of state, and government, motive forces and classes, parties, what will be the nature of the political system?

One of the most crucial questions would be related to the nature of ownership of means of production, exchange and information. Obviously, it is not going to be a socialism of the age of industrialism, of industrial means of production. Many basic changes in the means are taking place; more changes will take place in future. They are bound to bring about many transformations in the nature of the ownership of the means of production, exchange and services, a tricky question. This is a tricky, yet very important and crucial question.

Materialist Conception of History: Experiences and Lessons of Socialism

According to the materialist conception of history (also known as historical materialism), socio-economic formations or the different structures of society change to facilitate the growth of the productive forces. The means and forces of production, at a certain level of their development, conflict with the existing production relations, which change accordingly. This is known as revolution. The societies like the primitive, slave, feudal, etc. came and left the stage of history because of such an inherent contradiction in social motion. The same applies to the capitalist society.

Socialism too has the historical responsibility to facilitate and make way for growing productive forces, so as to enable a new society to emerge. If it does not do so, the socio-economic relations are likely to interfere with the development of society.

The socialist societies (countries), or 'models', as they are being called by some, helped the development of the productive forces in the beginning. But experience shows that with the passage of time, they began to prevent or restrict the growth of the productive forces. The state bureaucracy developed its own interests, as distinct from that of the society and the people.

The 'existing' socialism, and that which 'existed', has many lessons and experiences of socialist experiments. Often these experiments were simply subjective acts.

Socialism cannot be the result of subjective wishes. First and foremost, it is, and should be, an objective process. Socialism is a higher and superior stage of social development, as compared with capitalism. And the most important is that socialism should facilitate and assimilate the latest in the scientific and technological revolution.

But the fact is that the STR and the electronics revolution bypassed the socialist countries. Why? It is not that they did not have the technology and scientific knowledge. After all, the USSR led the space race for sometime. It was the first country to send the sputnik (satellite) into space. This is the same story in some other fields too (e.g. steel industry, machine making, etc.).

But the fact is that these technologies and sciences could not become a productive force. And one of the main reasons was that the state was highly bureaucratised and centralised. The state system and nature of society, where democracy was almost absent, where the ruling Party was only one, and it was cut off from the people, restricted the growth of the productive forces. Matters went to the extent where strange and ridiculous decrees were issued to prevent the use of certain things (even typewriters or copying machines, etc.) in the name of security.

So, electronics, computers and the STR in general could not become a *social force*.

Such knowledge was needed by the ruling bureaucracy (political force) but was not allowed to become social. Such a state of affairs led to the collapse of the socialist system or whatever variety of it. Its collapse cannot be explained by the acts of a few people or one person.

Basis of Marx's Concept of Socialism/Communism

Marx's concept was based, among others, on the large-scale production, growing larger. The factories and production were becoming larger and more concentrated, he said. Therefore, the contradictions between private ownership and social labour, becoming increasingly socialised, could not be sustained; they were bound to be torn asunder. The contradiction could be solved only through the establishment of social ownership of means of production, Marx said.

Today, many changes are taking place in this scenario. The main one is that the means of production and factories have stopped growing large and larger. The STR and electronics revolution has introduced new types of means of production. They are becoming smaller and more compact. This is a common tendency today. The STR has led to the creation of more efficient machines which can be run by a person or a small group of individuals.

So, what will the nature of ownership be while this tendency is in operation? This is one of the crucial questions.

STR and Reversal of Historical Tendency of Productive Forces: Role of Knowledge

The role of small producer and entrepreneur has increased. Not that the large-scale production has ceased to exist or that it is not being established at all. But the tendency is against large-scale production, which has been reversed.

Therefore, the question of ownership in the future socialism is rendered more complex. Straightaway state and big collective ownership may not be the clear-cut solution to the problem of ownership. In addition to nationalisation and state ownership, there would be a wide variety and wide sections of individual and group producers, who would need protection and encouragement from the socialist state and society. Obviously, social and collective ownership of the means of production cannot be a general feature of the future socialism, as it was visualised earlier.

A new and crucial factor for the future socialism is the information and communication revolution. In this context, there can be no universal formula for socialism. Information and means of information are reaching every individual. There can be and should be no state and collective interference in the operation, ownership and information, which would be an interference in the rights of individuals. This last point is very important.

Information and knowledge are becoming increasingly important, even crucial, factors of economy. Information cannot be owned; it can only be disseminated. Can there be a state or collective ownership in these fields? The means of information can be state-owned in large-scale operations (e.g. in railways, etc. Reservation in the country is already there). The socialist state would need centralised knowledge (computer, satellite, etc.) management for several aspects of communication, transport, production, and other purposes. So, a knowledge economy and management for economic and other purposes in favour of people would create a people-oriented knowledge/information network. Beginnings and outlines of such a system can already be seen in the present social system.

At the same time, information and knowledge, their system and material means work at the individual level. An electronic computerised system, with the unity of voice, data and image can operate at mobile and handset level, and even lower levels. The means of information have a tendency to grow smaller rapidly, mainly because of intra-atomic and inter-particular spaces, which are being filled up by new techniques.

Marxism, and Modern Natural Sciences and Technology

1. Michelson-Morley experiments towards the end of the 19th century and Max Planck's 'Tight Quanta' in 1900 signalled the end of the classical era in physics in particular and in sciences in general. These and other discoveries inaugurated an era of quantum

mechanics and Einsteinian relativity, as distinct from Newtonian laws of motion and relativity. Albert Einstein developed the Special Theory of Relativity in 1905 and General Theory of Relativity in 1916, thus replacing Newtonian relativity.

2. Quantum mechanics and relativity inaugurated a whole new era of quantum world and relativity. It also inaugurated a new worldview, developing and replacing the Newtonian/Cartesian worldview.
3. A host of scientists contributed to the development of the new sciences and new worldview. Photon and electromagnetic waves/particles were seen as unity of particles and waves. A single photon was discovered to have passed through two slits, producing an interference pattern on the next screen; yet closing of one slit produced a speck of particle on the same screen! Niels Bohr showed, in 1913, that electrons themselves were quantised, while Heisenberg developed the uncertainty principle, showing, in 1927, that velocity and place of a particle could not be determined at the same time. Eddington, Shroedinger, EPR (Einstein-Podolsky-Rosen) thought experiment, discussions between Einstein and Niels Bohr for almost 35 years on thought experiments around the quantum world and relativity, inaugurating new concepts of reality, objectivity and space and time, are key steps to the whole new world and its view. The dialectics of wave and particle and whole new world of transformations finally put the Newtonian/ industrial world and its concepts behind by developing them further in a qualitatively new context.
4. The birth of new physics and new sciences created controversies and discussions in other fields including

philosophy. The Newtonian/Cartesian worldview yielded place to the new ones based on new levels of motion.

5. Space and time acquired new dimensions. Space could be bended; even light was found to be bent in certain conditions, as was clear from the observations of the behaviour of light. Light defied Newtonian concepts of matter and motion. Energy had to be redefined.
6. Time became the most important, decisive and determining aspect.
7. These discoveries had a decisive impact on new modern industrial and post-industrial technologies. Science and technology was so far dependent on the visible and the tangible, i.e. 'natural' forces and events. For the first time, the 'unnatural' that is 'not naturally occurring' forces became the basis of the development of production, science, thought, notions, concepts and equipment of daily life and of the conceptual world, with its new instruments of knowledge. Philosophy stood on the verge of giant, unprecedented transformations.
8. The old world was gone, a new one began. There was a complete upsurge, with nothing of the old science fitting the new reality. Scientists took some time to understand this, as also philosophers. But when they did come to terms with them, they inaugurated new science and technology.
9. Conflict between the naturally occurring society and its naturally occurring means of living came into conflict with the new instruments, tools and means of knowledge and production, which took on the form of new means of information. Time and space collapsed also in the domain of society. It became increasingly difficult to explain scientific, technological

and social events with the Newtonian worldview. The new worldview has to be intensely dialectical and instant.

10. Hegelian dialectics has come to the fore, as never before. Lenin said nobody can become a real Marxist without mastering Hegel. This is more applicable to the present-day events and instant transformations. Motion is not just the unity of 'this and that'; it is 'this as well as that'. Motion is not at this place this instant, at another at another moment. Motion and dialectics is 'at this point and not at this point' at the same moment. The quantum revolution has brought this out into the open, in contrast to the industrial motions.
11. Philosophy should master the method of 'this is and is not'.
12. Quantum philosophy is a new phase in the development of philosophy, which needs to be mastered by Marxism. Relativity and quantum concepts need to be assimilated in the Marxist philosophy. Increasing velocities, that is, rapidly accelerating 'time' is producing accelerating transformations in humans, society, thought and philosophies. Time is becoming more and more decisive with the coming out of the quantum forces into the open, particularly as the means of production and communication.
13. Human/computer interface, particularly brain/ computer interface contain far-reaching implications for the matter/idea relationship. Processes, including thought processes, are being zeroed in and pinpointed to the particulate and wave levels. Thought can be 'seen', particularised, 'identified'! This is an absolutely new level of development of material motion.

14. Genes, chemical reactions, brain functions, etc. can be and are being reduced to, becoming explainable, through particulate motions and structures. The particle is becoming the centre and basis of notions, whether within the atom or out in space.
15. The earth is surrounded more and more by consciousness in the form of internet, a variety of objective consciousness, created by the subject. Great implications.
16. New aspects of subject/object relationship are coming out. The subject can be constituted, decentred and reconstituted.
17. The world of the virtual reality is particularly relevant here, where one can 'create' and uncreate the reality at will. New aspects of 'reality' as apparent from the discussions of Einstein, Niels Bohr and Eddington as also Karl Popper.
18. Nanotechnology and superconductivity have the potentials to completely transform the existing concepts to the unprecedented new qualitative levels. They contain the seeds of the liberation of the individual, in consonance with that of the society.
19. Human thinking stands on the verge of new thought levels. Marxism has to catch up with it in order to remain at the horizon of 'frontier thinking', as it has always been. Otherwise it may fall behind the quantum speeds and levels.
20. We are living in the most exciting era of giant transformations and upheavals in matter, motion, time, and thought. We should accept this pleasant challenge and reach new levels of abstraction, thought and practice

21. We are today able to look at ourselves out from space by going out into space or by sitting at home, seeing ourselves as a planet and humanity, as new unity in tangible form. It shows that we can overcome all our contradictions and exist as a member of the solar system. This is a new level of consciousness. We can now philosophise as humanity.
22. We can, in this context and from this vantage point, look at and solve the problems of the great environmental crisis of natural degradation and protection of human beings and of life itself.
23. Humans and their thoughts will never be the same again. They stand on the verge of a giant universal renewal.

Future Technologies and Socialism/Communism

Therefore, the individuals and groups will have an equally important role, may be even greater role in socialism and communism. After all, a computer or a mobile almost acts like a whole office. Technologies are now proceeding to the nano-scales.

The rapidly changing composition of society brings about a transformation in the context, composition and methods of socialism. There is a growing opposition of world imperialism, in particular of US imperialism. Giant MNCs and spread of finance capital present new challenges.

In such a context, the movement towards socialism acquires a broad front. Socialism will have to present a better and more attractive alternative to mature capitalism, which some people also term as late capitalism. Socialism should be looking after the interest of the broadest sections of population. It cannot be the socialism of the older type. Here, therefore, the concept of socialism as the collective and state ownership of the means of production, as such, cannot apply. Emergence of the means of information further complicate the matter. All the productive and distributive sections, classes and individuals have to be involved.

Socialism does not mean all-out socialisation of the means of production and information, nor centralised control alone. The matter should be decided by the society and by the socialist democratic system. This has to be borne in mind. Socialism does mean progressive suspension and elimination of the capitalist laws, but not mechanically and subjectively. The process has to be objectively necessitated, and only with the consent of the people, with the plurality of parties and organisations. It cannot be imposed and centrally directed.

Socialism of the future has to be a highly flexible, democratic system, superior to capitalism in every respect that will open the gates for full-scale development and unleashing of the means of production and information.

It will be a socialism, different in most respects from what existed and exists so far.

2

Socialism in the 21st Century

M. Vijaya Kumar

1. Socialism in the 21st Century

It is said that neither is *Das Kapital* a "Book of Genesis", nor is Lenin a St. Augustine. Marxism is a science that needs constant efforts at rejuvenation, updating and course correction, just like any other branch of science. Socialism may be a historical *possibility*, or even *necessary* to eliminate the evils of capitalism, but this does not mean that it will *inevitably* take its place. We are not passengers waiting for the train of socialism to arrive so that we can board it and enjoy the journey. We are revolutionaries, fighting to make socialism a reality.

We have to formulate our ideas about the 21st century socialism that is adapted to our historical, social, cultural, and political context, not in an unorganised and chaotic way, but by taking advantage of the tools and the framework of references that Marxism-Leninism gives us. There are a few ideas that spring from our consciousness when we think of socialism of the future. First of all, it must be profoundly democratic. As Chavez said, "One of the determining factors of 21st century socialism must be participatory democracy and popular power; everything has to be centred in the people. The party must be subordinated to the people, not the other way around." A society dominated by an all-powerful state does not produce human beings who can create socialism. For the same reason, socialism is not populism. Rosa Luxemburg insisted that the requirement of "socialist democracy begins simultaneously with the beginnings of the destruction of class rule and the construction of socialism." Socialist democracy is not to be conceived as applying merely to the political sphere, but would have to extend to all aspects of public and private life. Meszaros emphasised the need for a more radical democratic socialist revolution that would put the people in charge.

Objectives

What type of society do we want to build? This question may appear very vague, involving a series of abstract ideas:

- Human development as the core component
- Satisfaction of communal needs and purposes
- Democratic participation in all sectors of collective life, priority to the use of renewable natural resources
- Predominance of use value on exchange value
- Socialising markets
- Parallelism to bypass the wasteful, corrupt and often hostile bureaucracies
- Subsidiarity (favouring local production)
- Interculturality
- Knowledge management of the whole society for meeting societal needs.

Socialism had to be built from the bottom up rather than from the top down. Instead of centralised planning by a remote bureaucracy there could be decentralised democratic planning using advanced information technology. It is a society in which the explicit goal is not the growth of capital or of the material means of production but, rather, human development itself—the growth of human capacities. Istvan Meszaros in *Beyond Capital*, stressed the importance of building a new communal system of production and consumption—one in which there is an exchange of activities determined by communal needs and communal purposes.

We have to get rid of the myth that there is something sacred about large-scale production for the national and international market. We have to begin thinking of creating small enterprises which produce food, goods and services for the local market, that is, for our communities. Instead of destroying the skills of workers, which is what large-scale industry does, these small enterprises will combine craftsmanship, or the preservation and enhancement of human skills, with the new technologies which make possible flexible production and constant readjustment to serve the needs of local customers.

It is in a rich atmosphere of discussion that the revolutionary party must function, for this alone can provide a check against its going horribly wrong in its assessment of the present. Marxism-Leninism is a living, developing tool that can analyse new conditions and questions. Communist ideology advances amidst a turbulent process. New understandings must overcome the inertia of past ways of looking at things, and correct and incorrect viewpoints must be sorted out. A correct relationship between the State and the Party in a socialist society is an absolute must.

As Prakash Karat says: "To build socialism, particularly in less developed capitalist countries is a more protracted and complex process than it was envisaged under the impact of the October Revolution. The sobering and hard lesson for the future is that the absence of democracy in any socialist experiment, the failure to expand and develop the potential of democracy will deform and distort socialism."

Miguel Figueroa, Communist Party of Canada writes, "On the basis of analysis and discussion, the Canadian Communist party placed special emphasis on our evolving conception of socialism, particularly with respect to the democratic content of socialist construction and development. But we also reaffirmed what we believe to be the essential aspects or features of the socialist alternative, namely: (1) that although socialism can and must involve all social forces that can be united in its construction, *the process must be led by the working class and its political representatives*; (2) that the socialist alternative must be deeply imbued with the principles of *equality, social justice and internationalism*; (3) that the working class and its allies have the *democratic right and also the responsibility to defend socialism* in the face of resistance from its class enemies—domestic and external; and (4) that the economic foundation of socialism must be based on the *systematic transformation by degrees of ownership relations from private to social*. In fact, the term "by degrees" comes directly from the *Communist Manifesto* itself."

2. India's Path to Socialism

India is a land of small farmers, with 65 crores of her 110 crore people living on the land and 80 per cent small farmers. In other words, the land provides livelihood security for 65 per cent of the people, and the small farmers provide food security for 110 crores. Without small farmers, India will be a food insecure, violent and undemocratic society. Agricultural reforms that are being introduced are actually aimed at destroying the production capacity of the farm lands and would lead to further marginalisation of the farming communities. Contract farming has become the new agricultural mantra. Private companies enter agriculture with the specific objective of garnering more profits from the same piece of land. Allowing direct procurement of farm commodities, setting up special markets for the private companies to mop up the produce, and to set up land share companies, are all directed at the uncontrolled entry of the multinational corporations in the farm sector. Farming has moved into the hands of agribusiness corporations and monopoly retail chains are taking over. Ultimately this will drive out a majority of the 60 crore farmers out of agriculture. Ruthlessly, each policy, every budget moves us further towards a corporate takeover of agriculture. The McKinsey-authored Vision 2020 set out the removal of millions of people from the land as one of its objectives. Successive governments at the Centre and in many states seem to have latched on to that vision with great zeal. This is not a natural evolutionary process. It is a violent and imposed process. The industrial model of farming is at the root of farmers' suicides. Yet, the disease is being offered as a cure. The Agriculture Minister, Sharad Pawar has stated that farmers need to be "weaned" off the land. And the Vice Chairman of the Planning Commission, Montek Singh Ahluwalia has talked of "the feasibility of large corporate ownership of farmland." Since the reform process has started in China, 20 crores of people have shifted to cities. In India, the ruling classes claim that agriculture accounts for only 22 per cent of the nation's gross domestic product (GDP) while as much as 70 per cent live in rural areas. So the cure they suggest is that about 50 crore of people have to seek other avenues of sustenance. With no opportunities in rural areas, all these 50 crores have to migrate to cities. That will be a disaster for the country's economy.

Which Way for the Reforms?

There is an old saying that if you don't know where you want to go, then any road will take you there. Our experience tells us that if you don't know where you want to go, then no road will take you there. Our greatest failing is that we have lost sight of an alternative. Because of our failure to envisage an alternative as a whole, we have many small pieces, many small 'no's; indeed, the only feasible alternative to barbarism proposed has been barbarism with a human face. Let us think about a real alternative to barbarism, a grand conception but yet a very simple one.

The Left in India has stopped talking about a socialist society that can replace the neoliberal economy. Mostly, we hear them talking about improvements to the present policies. The magnitude of reforms has no meaning unless the direction is clear. It is imperative that the left has to put forward an alternate agenda for development and modernisation.

Anti-Capitalist Path of Development on the Way to a Socialist Society

A few important steps that can be taken to take India towards a non-capitalist path of development are listed here:

1. Recognise and respect the inalienable and non-negotiable rights of peoples and communities to their land, forest and water resources. Keep water and water services out of the WTO and all other trade negotiations and agreements. The solution lies in communitisation of our water resources, not privatisation or corporatisation.
2. The inter-linking of water bodies and water management and conservation should be undertaken in a bottoms-up approach, with the task of building and maintaining irrigation and water conservation projects entrusted to local bodies. By bringing about more area of waste land to use, we can distribute land to the landless poor, help them to set up agricultural cooperatives that provide a safety net against adverse

weather conditions and consequent crop failures, distribute fertilisers, pesticides and agricultural machinery and market their products. Local educated talent will have enormous opportunities in running such ventures. Agricultural reforms will be meaningful only when aided by such measures.

3. We need to tackle water resources management issues at the local level with supporting legislation and intermediate-level institutions (basin, macro-watershed or district, etc.). Participatory watershed development has proved to be an attractive approach to rural development over recent decades.
4. To take the path of decentralised water management and energy planning with maximum use of renewable energy sources to meet the energy needs of peoples and communities equitably. To come forward and involve the people in a democratic, transparent, accountable debate and discussion in planning and decision-making of water, land and other natural resources.
5. Undertake economic, social, cultural and health impact assessments of dams and related projects. Undertake country level review of performance of large dams. Inter basin transfers should be attempted only after there has been a total scientific effort to conserve and use the water available in the basin itself.
6. While appreciating the existing programmes of water harvesting by government and non-government agencies, it is suggested that a systematic scientific approach should be made mandatory in the selection and the location of the harvesting structures followed by a systematic monitoring of its utility aspects.
7. India has 50 crores of young people. Out of 70 crores of working age population, only 48 crores

are employed in some sort of occupation and the rest are without any regular and reliable source of income. Unemployment is rising nationwide. In the entire country, the rate of unemployment has gone up from 13.9% in 1980 to 18.2% in 2000. There are 5 crores unemployed youth registered in employment exchanges and many more than this number who do not have regular employment. Nearly half the working age population lack employment of any sort. Employment in the unorganised sector accounts for 91.39% of the workforce.

8. India brings out 20 lakh professional graduates into the workforce annually. Out of this, only 20% are able to get employment. The IT industry employs only 0.02% of the total workforce.
9. Employment as a whole, has suffered during the period of liberalisation. According to the Government's own calculations, employment growth has fallen from 2.7 per cent a year in the pre-liberalisation period to just over 1% a year in the liberalisation period. Today, thanks to the liberalisation policies, the job growth rate is a mere 0.5%.
10. Fifty per cent of the total workforce is employed in agriculture. The major cause of the collapse of employment as a whole is the zero growth in agricultural employment (0.02% per year). Lacking opportunities, crores of people are migrating to cities seeking a livelihood.
11. India's land bank is about 75–80 crore acres. Out of this, 50 crore acres can be potentially farmed, but today only 30–35 crore acres are arable and used for agriculture. More than 70 crore people rely on this land base for their survival. We need to bring the remaining 15 crore acres into productive use. Land reforms have

to be implemented so that the rural poor can survive and convert this surplus land to agriculture.

12. Agriculture is the main base of the Indian economy. But, sadly, investment in agriculture, already very low, has been declining to dangerously low levels.
13. Bank loans to poor peasants are drying up. In the last 15 years, bank loans to poor farmers have fallen by 88 per cent. Credit is needed for water, for fertilisers, for pesticides, even for seeds. Institutional credit at reasonable interest rates is not available. Poor peasants have no other option but to take money from loan sharks and are unable to repay; 2 lakh farmers have committed suicide in the last 15 years.
14. In our country, 2,17,000 villages have water quality problems. Excess fluoride, arsenic, nitrate, iron and salinity are causing health hazards. Only 55% of villages are connected by roads. On the other hand, the ever-growing urban poor, surviving in slums, are being continuously pushed into darkness by slum demolition drives, neglected in sanitation, power, and water.
15. The establishment of SEZs is not the only and necessary way to industrialisation. We have to apply industrialisation that can create employment, not simply profits for the rich.
16. Out of the tax concessions given to the rich industrialists (nearly 1.5 lakh crores per year), only one-third of this amount, that is 50 thousand crores is sufficient to provide gainful employment to the unemployed youth of this country.
17. In fact the Indian economy has become further distorted due to neoliberal reforms in such a fashion that the conventional measures of its 'growth' do not necessarily represent a better life for the vast majority

of the people. The only solution lies in creating jobs in the rural areas and increasing investments in agro-based industries. This can only ease the acute unemployment situation.

18. To increase the employment, the approach plan to the Eleventh Plan asserts that we must pay special attention to labour-intensive manufacturing sectors such as the food processing industry, textiles, small and medium enterprises, tourism and construction.
19. Decentralise power and empower local bodies. All public works in rural areas should be given to work cooperatives set up by unemployed youth. Gram Sabhas should decide what kind of projects should be undertaken, so that people get the infrastructure they need.
20. The present systems to administer the country's resources are primitive and inefficient. Both the prevention and cure of this disease is possible only if we allow technology to take precedence over the norm. This however does not mean that technology by itself can make governments transparent, smart and responsive as there are a host of other factors that influence governance. Only the creation of a knowledge and information economy can create opportunities and thereby prosperity to impoverished areas.
21. Undertake integrated study and assessment of human and material resources, based on the concept of knowledge hubs, at national, state, regional and area level, by combining the potential of GIS, IT, meteorological and historical data and plan for economic growth based on water resources development as the core. Distributed power generation using locally available resources and managed locally is increasingly being seen as a more effective and environmentally friendly alternative.

22. Our emphasis on IT initiative has to shift from cheap contract work for export to the development of high quality inward looking software and IT services that are specifically designed for India's development needs.
23. Spurious IT training centres are looting the youth. The certificates issued by them are worthless. The government should certify the IT Training Institutes, prescribe the syllabus and conduct common examinations and issue degrees and diplomas.
24. IT can be used for improving agricultural productivity and this creates more opportunities for the educated jobless in rural areas.
25. IT should be used to make the handicrafts sector more productive and thereby create better income opportunities for youth.
26. We need lakhs of computer professionals to work for India's IT needs in areas such as satellite mapping, tax collection, traffic and crime control, E-governance, education system, public health care, bio-technology and so many other fields.
27. We want the talent of Indian youth to be used for India's development, not America's profits. For every dollar invested in India, American companies take back 10 dollars. Our slogan is "We want hi-tech jobs in rural areas".
28. IT can be used in India to transform the country by providing a new vision to the youth of the country, enabling them to stand up, no longer feeling inferior to others in the world. We can deploy the talents of the vast multitude of India's IT manpower to empower India's development, instead of working for others.

The youth and student organisations should launch a massive movement "IT4India" to demand implementation of these demands, calling on the youth and students who genuinely want this country to break the shackles of poverty, corruption, under development and unemployment. Let us together usher in a new India by united struggles for equality, social and economic justice and an end to exploitation.

3. The Changing Nature of Work and Role of Labour

'Why is it that every time I hire a pair of hands I get a human being as well?'—Henry Ford

New Technologies and Work

The spread of computers and electronic means of communication has significantly influenced the mode of work with a shift away from centralised workplaces. For example, the much-publicised reengineering of capitalist enterprises has encouraged the outsourcing of activities once performed in-house. Companies now rely more and more on outside service providers and suppliers. The evolution of an ever-more complex technical division of labour has created a constantly changing demand for an extremely diverse range of skills. But the fact is that a developing country such as India has a very small formal sector. About 92 per cent of the workforce is employed in the informal sector, with little or insignificant impact of modern technologies. The increased precariousness of their jobs, often as contract jobs, makes it even harder for them to seek improvements in their pay and working conditions; it in fact degrades the living conditions every day. In the formal sector, a flattening of certain internal corporate hierarchies does not mean that the overall distance separating workers and employers is lessened. The lean workplace is one in which constant stress is placed upon the workers through speeding up assembly lines, reducing the number of workers, and taking away materials, while the workers are expected to complete production targets to get their performance-linked wages. The truth is that in the most fundamental sense, i.e. social relations, there is nothing new at all about today's economy. But capitalism itself is never at rest. The competitive dynamic at the heart of the system abhors all fixed routine. No sooner has it established one method of production, and the labour discipline necessary for it to function, than it uproots it in favour of a more profitable alternative. In the process, they seek to take back all that has been won by the working class by their hard won struggles. The imposition of capitalist control over the work process is never complete. Class struggle is written into the very foundation of capitalist society. Capitalist relations of production exploit technology to find new ways of controlling and replacing labour.

Working Class Consciousness

Working class consciousness is never simply either wholly pro-capitalist or wholly anti-capitalist, but taken as a whole, it is always a 'contradictory consciousness'. Many arguments are put forth that in the knowledge economy of the 21st century, class is no longer a key concept, and class conflict is no longer a central issue. They tell us that Marxism is no longer relevant. This contradictory consciousness, described best by Italian Marxist Antonio Gramsci, is composed of two broad streams. One is what Gramsci called 'common sense—the day-to-day ideology of the bourgeoisie'. This is the inherited ideology of the existing society, notions of deference and respect for the rich and famous, individualism, prejudices of caste, religion and so on. The other is 'good sense'. These are the received and learnt ideas of solidarity, resistance, comradeship, equality, democracy, unity in struggle, and organisation that form part of the culture of the labour movement. Good sense is largely the accumulated intellectual inheritance of the history of working class struggle and its generalisation in the form of Marxist theory. From this it follows that outbursts of struggle, of strikes, political mass movements and revolutions are just as important at the beginning of the 21st century as in the past.

Three Questions Before the Working-Class at the Dawn the of 21st Century:

- What changes in the economy and in the process of work have taken place that affect the working class, in terms of their abilities to organise, mobilise, and be effective?
- What is our analysis of the current domestic and international situation in general, but specifically, the situation facing workers?
- What is the nature of international working class solidarity in the 21st century?

4. Problems of Building Socialism in the 21st Century

Learning from the failures of post-revolutionary societies, the revolutionaries in Venezuela say: "We are creating an economy at the service of human beings instead of human beings at the service of the economy." This is the essence of the socialist goal. It may well represent the hopes of billions of people. Socialism cannot arrive overnight—the road to such a major transformation of social structure and people's consciousness is indeed very long. It is also full of pitfalls. "Throughout this stage, the class struggle between the bourgeoisie and the proletariat goes on and the question of 'who will win' between the roads of capitalism and socialism remains, as does the danger of restoration of capitalism." (Mao Zedong, 1964)

The Experience of the Soviet Union

Many factors underlie the failure to establish a socialist society in the Soviet Union, mainly the development of a privileged bureaucratic elite and a distorted nationalism. The Soviet system produced its own contradictions: a bureaucratic structure which operated far removed from the masses and was so rigid and entrenched that it could sabotage economic and political reforms designed to improve the efficiency of production and distribution. The shortcomings of the Soviet economy were not a result of the failure of central planning, but the way planning was conducted. Soviet political culture was defined by the bureaucratic-authoritarian deformation.

According to Sitaram Yechury: "The extreme centralisation of power in the socialist societies, which were characterised by a dictatorship of the Party and which ultimately ended up de-politicising the working class to a significant extent." We can sum up as follows:

1. Soviet society was indeed socialist.
2. This society had many undesirable and problematic features.
3. The problems of Soviet society were in part historical as well as systemic.
4. We must reflect carefully on the lessons to be learned from this failure.
5. Other forms of Marxian socialism are possible.

Com. Sam Webb, the chairman of the Communist Party USA explains the conventional view of the communist movement as follows:

- After the revolution, the period of consolidation would be relatively brief and new forms of popular power would emerge.
- The state would acquire more functions and extend

its reach into new areas of social, cultural, and civic life, including control of the mass media.

- That market relations would quickly give way to centralised planning and a completely socialised economy.
- Socialist state property would be clearly dominant and would eventually become the singular form of ownership.

These assumptions have to be revisited and revised in view of experience and new theoretical insights. As for the economy, the main issue is not whether we would employ market mechanisms, but rather the issue is to what extent and for how long? I would expect that the economy would be a mixed one, combining different forms of socialist and cooperative property as well as space, within clear limits, for private enterprise. While democratic planning would begin to play a role in organising economic life, market mechanisms would probably operate over sectors of the socialised economy for much longer than we thought years ago. The costs of the reproduction of labour power would be socialised as much as possible and the narrowing of economic equalities would be a paramount goal of a socialist society.

5. Dialectical Materialism and Modern Science

Marxism and Science

According to Lenin, dialectical materialism sees all scientific thought as a "series of successive approximations to the truth". J.D. Bernal says, "Marxism transforms science and gives it greater scope and significance". For Bernal the humanistic and the scientific dimensions were one. As Bernal saw in the transition to the future, scientific and socialist philosophical thinking plays a key role as dialectics permeates all of physics. The goals of human freedom and ecological sustainability are inseparable and necessitate for their advancement the building of Socialism for the 21st century, according to John Bellamy Foster, editor of *Monthly Review*.

Marxism is a democratic form of rationality, one that believes not in the logical purity of eternal Reason but in the logical potential of democratic reasoning. However, we should not be under the false premise that the scientific character of Marxism depends on its ability to predict the future. Rather, Marxism, as a method of analysis and materialist world outlook, has uncovered laws that govern socio-economic and political processes. Science under capitalism develops without any ultimate philosophic foundation and without any unifying principle. Whereas Marxism provides the basis for ontological principles and particular scientific concepts to mutually correct and modify each other. Dialectical thought has certainly shaped many of the new inventions and discoveries, by guiding the scientists to the correct path in their quest for truth. Discoveries and inventions in science, such as genetics, cosmology and particle physics enrich dialectical and historical materialism by constant undulation and enrichment. Let us briefly discuss a few developments in science that have proven the relevance of Dialectical Materialism beyond doubt.

Relativity and Quantum Mechanics

Quantum mechanics has given scientists and engineers a new and deeper understanding of physical reality. In conjunction with the other great breakthrough of 20th century physics, Einstein's theory of relativity, it leads to the possibility of enormous advances in human society. But the conservative academics who developed quantum mechanics inserted into the subject a direct attack on the philosophical basis of Marxism —dialectical materialism—by denying the existence of physical reality. It is argued that physical reality only exists as a result of the act of observation. But Marxists say that instead of disputing reality, quantum mechanics validates the dialectical position of development in nature. At the quantum level, the dialectical contradiction is embodied in the wave-particle duality of matter, which is neither unnatural nor unreal.

Chaos and Dialectics

In complex, non-linear systems, a small change in the input could produce a huge change in the output. The chaos theory sets definite limits to the predictability of complex non-linear systems. However, scientists are groping in the direction of a dialectical view of nature, as they comprehend the interdependence of various elements and living beings. Marxism applies itself to perhaps the most complex of all non-linear systems—human society.

Marxism and Darwinism

Modern evolutionists want to prove that there are no leaps either in nature or in history. Dialectics, on the other hand, knows full well that in nature and also in human thought and history leaps are inevitable. Stephen Jay Gould argues that the evolution of intelligent life is accidental. It is not some smooth, gradual movement from lower to higher. It proceeds with leaps and jumps, punctuated with long periods of steady, gradual development; there are breaks, retrogressions, and pauses within the general progress of evolution. There is no reason to suppose that evolution has reached its limit, or that human beings will experience no further development. The process of evolution will continue, although it will not necessarily take the same form as in the past. Profound changes in the social environment, including genetic engineering, can modify the process of natural selection, giving human beings for the first time the possibility of determining their own evolution, at least to some degree. This will open up an entirely new chapter in human development, especially in a society guided by the free and conscious decisions of men and women, and not the blind play of market forces and the animal struggle for survival.

Social Darwinism

Homo Economicus, a concept which is the byproduct of Social Darwinism; symbolises the archetypical ideal capitalist, rational and cold-blooded in decision-making for his own sake. Social Darwinism promotes the view that laissez-faire capitalism is the most "natural" of all possible economic systems and that the human race would be best served by allowing poor people to perish rather than helping them survive.

Developments and Distortions in Marxist Philosophy in the 20th Century

In the 20th century there are endless interpretations of the "philosophy of Marx", from the interior of the Marxist movement as well as in its exterior. The theories of Marxism in the social sphere have been the decisive factor in the development of modern social sciences. For Marx and Engels, literature is not merely a passive reflection of the economic base. But Georg Lukacs conceived ideology and literature as components of the superstructure and must correspond to the economic base of society. The Italian theorist Antonio Gramsci, with his concept of hegemony, allows for an even more flexible reading of the base/ superstructure model. Gramsci believes that ideology alone cannot explain the extent to which people are willing to accept dominant values.

In a way, Gramsci's notion of hegemony is a continuation of the concepts behind ideology. Literature, then, may be seen as something that both reinforces dominant values and occasionally calls them into question. Whereas Althusser suggests that ideology and hegemony, like literature, present a constructed version of reality, one which does not necessarily reflect the actual conditions of life.

There is a general tendency to be observed, like that of the Frankfurt School, whose initial purpose was to apply Marxism to the 20th century and finally ended up as anti-Marxist, by progressively shedding class struggle, and putting too much stress on the awareness of the individual. Trends such as Multi-Culturalism, De-Constructionism, Critical Theory, Feminism and Postmodernism had all traversed this path and had taken their inspiration from the Frankfurt School. Frederick Jameson has argued that postmodernism is the "cultural logic of late capitalism". Postmodernism has today degenerated into the philosophy of the neo-conservatives, who believe they can counter Marxism by rejecting ideologies.

Marxism shares with consistent scientific method and rationalism the belief in the concreteness of truth, and the provisional hypothetical nature of scientific theory. Materialist dialectics presents the historical fact that humanity has conquered nature through knowing it more accurately. The progress of the productive forces—from stone tools to the internet—has occurred because of the interaction between human thought, consciousness, and the objective world.

Marxists defend science, rationality, the idea of an objective, knowable world and human subjectivity—but we do so critically, from the standpoint of dialectical materialism. It is only Marxism which can provide a coherent critique of "meta-narratives" where they serve as justification for oppression and has been the only theory that did not give an inch to them, and the only force which combated them effectively in practice.

6. Decentralisation and Empowerment

Denning Decentralisation

We can define decentralisation as a process of transferring responsibilities and resources from the decision-making top towards intermediate or base levels. Even with its potential for democratisation and de-bureaucratisation, decentralisation is far from being a formula for the solution of the basic problems of contemporary societies. Neoliberal decentralisation can only lead, and in practice has led, to the strengthening of the existing power structures, a technocratic centralisation policy and a deepening power asymmetry between ever-weaker Third World countries and stronger transnational blocs. For Oscar Lange, the centralisation/decentralisation relation constituted a basic dilemma for socialism. The market is a mechanism too powerful to be considered as a docile instrument of socialist advance. We must plan for and bring about a society capable of avoiding the omnipresence of a powerful central bureaucracy. The goal of socialism is inseparable from democracy, and democracy means, among others things, the right of common people to participate in the decision-making process, to decide how to participate and to control their own lives and destinies.

Empowerment of the People

One of the biggest problems of a socialist transition and transformation is how to overcome society's hierarchical structure in the process of transferring class power to the people. Empowerment applies to all domains and to all levels of society.

7. Socialism and the Market and the Role of Planning

The theoretical basis for a new socialism: The principal bases for a 21st century socialism must be radical democracy and efficient planning. Central planning of some kind (along with local and regional planning initiatives) is certainly a necessity for socialism and its greatest economic tool. In fact, planning, if emerging from the active participation of the population, is probably the only effective means for democratic participation in economic decisions and for the fulfilment of genuine popular needs. It is the fulfilment of such needs and the active, democratic involvement of the population in their fulfilment that are most important. In a socialist economy markets will continue to play a role, but as a servant rather than master. Socialism led by the associated producers must seek to turn the enormous productivity of modern society to other ends than the accumulation of capital.

The Soviet Experience

The crisis of the Soviet political culture does not mean there was a crisis in the institutions of socialist planning and management. A general model of socialism can be synthesised from the entire 20th century experience. That model has at its centre a system of democratic planning, with evolving market relations surrounding it, combining central with decentral planning.

Socialism with Chinese Characteristics

The Chinese version of socialist market economy is characterised as the primary stage of socialism in transition employing market guidance. They argue: "The socialist market economy is designed for transition from an early capitalist or even pre-capitalist society and the focus is to create the prerequisites for socialism." Using the "classical" theories of Marxism-Leninism the socialist market economy as practiced in China will not appear to be socialist. Having a strong state sector does not equate with socialism. Reform in China and Vietnam includes, among other changes, a shift away from the predominance of bureaucratic coordination towards predominance of market coordination. According to Prabhat Patnaik, "Market socialism" is a contradiction in terms, a negation of socialism (from which it follows that the concept of "socialist commodity production" which China has been talking about of late is equally untenable, though the idea of using markets for certain specific purposes in socialist societies is not). In order to develop a viable 21st century alternative we must insist that a socialism that loses its soul will not regain it later. The Chinese experience suggests that this leads inexorably back to capitalism.

Martin Hart-Landsberg and Paul Burkett in their book *China and Socialism* say: "It is our position that China's market reforms have led not to socialist renewal but rather to full-fledged capitalist restoration, including growing foreign economic domination." Significantly, this outcome was driven by more than simple greed and class interest. Once the path of pro-market reforms was embarked upon, each subsequent step in the reform process was largely driven by tensions and contradictions generated by the reforms themselves. The weakening of central planning led to ever more reliance on market and profit incentives, which in turn encouraged the privileging of private enterprises over state enterprises and, increasingly, of foreign enterprises and markets over domestic ones. Although a correct understanding of the dynamics of China's reform process supports the Marxist position that market socialism is an unstable formation, this important insight has largely been lost because of the continuing widespread belief by many progressives that China remains in some sense a socialist country. The rapid economic growth that accompanied the reforms was largely due to factors other than efficiency gains from marketisation and privatisation. The arguments in this book undercut the widespread image of wise Chinese policymakers carefully and deliberately engineering a relatively stable, low-cost transition to a more productive market-driven regime. China's foreign investment driven, export-led growth cannot be treated as simply a positive sum experience replicable by other nations.

Al L. Sargis, the Director of the Centre for Marxist Education of CPUSA lists a few considerations for socialist market economy:

1. How does the public sector remain strong enough to be competitive with the capitalist sector in the market?
2. While state enterprises control the "commanding heights" do these "heights" vary in accordance with historical conditions?
3. How does the state deal with the negative phenomena produced by the market economy?
4. How does the working class maintain the path towards socialism over several generations of transition?
5. Does the scope of the state and market alter as the socialist market economy reaches the threshold of socialism proper and what role, if any, does the market play after this plateau has been reached?

Issues of this sort reflect the urgent problems facing the concrete test of political practice in the countries currently constructing socialism via a socialist market economy.

On the Question of State Ownership and the Transition to Socialism

Firstly, state ownership of industry by and of itself is not socialism. Secondly: "Given the complexity of an industrial society, it is neither possible, nor is it desirable, to govern all decision-making from a single centre. Consequently, we have to seek to reconcile global planning with a measure of free initiative for market forces within the same economy. Nationalisation and state ownership (even under workers' control) does not of itself resolve the problem of effective planning.

On the Issue of Planning

The scientific and technological revolution makes it possible to project a new kind of socialist future that was not foreseeable till now. The technological basis of previous planning efforts needs to be placed in its proper context. Today, the large monopolies effectively use "just in time" production technologies and techniques to instantaneously adjust production targets and product lines consistent with consumer preferences. We have to examine how such techniques could be implemented to strengthen the efficiency of socialist forms of planning. These aims can best be met through a cooperative, planned form of social economy under a radically democratic political constitution. Modern computer technology would have little difficulty in modelling the whole country's production and consumption needs. A system of costing things in terms of labour time is not just an acceptable idea, it is also practical using modern computer technology. The computation of labour values for a whole economy is now feasible in a few minutes using modern supercomputers.

Basic Concepts of Planning

We need a characterisation of socialist economic planning which centres on the capacity of the planning system to impose democratically decided objectives on the course of economic development.

Levels of Planning

Planning decisions may be broken down into three levels: macroeconomic planning, strategic planning, and detailed production planning.

Macroeconomic planning sets certain general parameters governing the evolution of the economy over time.

Strategic planning concerns the changing industrial structure of the economy.

Detailed production planning concerns the precise allocation of resources.

Strategic Planning

1. The planning of the industrial structure
2. Environmental considerations
3. Investment planning and the time dimension of production
4. Planning of the mode of distribution of goods and services
5. Agricultural production planning

Detailed Planning: Effective detailed planning requires a standardised system of product identification, which in turn demands sophisticated computer databases.

The Marketing of Consumer Goods: Setting prices at market-clearing levels in each period, and then using the gap between these prices and labour content as a signal for increasing or reducing production in the next period.

Planning and Information: A system of computerised planning which involves the simulation of the behaviour of the economy in great detail.

8. Socialist Knowledge Economy

In order to avoid technological determinism and idealism,

one should see the information or knowledge "revolution" as part and parcel of a new form of techno-capitalism. In a knowledge economy, knowledge plays a key role in the economic value addition across all sectors of the economy. The knowledge economy concept being touted by neoliberals is fraught with contradictions, which are self-defeating. The roots of modern informational problems lies in the basic tension between the communal character of information and the hierarchical, exploitative, and private character of capitalist relations. A true knowledge economy is one in which the fruits of knowledge effort are deployed for the benefit of the entire population, for improving their living conditions—not for enriching a few—because knowledge is a social product and it can never be privately owned. Moreover, intense human effort is required to process information and to turn it into useful knowledge. Such knowledge should not be owned by a few individuals. A common but incorrect presumption was that new technology would generally democratise work automatically. Real change is not that painless.

In an industrial economy, which I prefer to call a raw material processing economy, economic activity has to be centralised spatially under a command structure with strict hierarchy to achieve economies of scale. This is reversed in a knowledge economy. In a knowledge economy, economy activity can be highly dispersed and broken up into independent cellular units. This makes the economic operation more efficient and cost-effective. Concentrating all activities under one private corporation runs counter to the very logic of a knowledge economy. That is why, capitalism and knowledge economy are incompatible. Deploying India's IT and tech manpower for its own needs will be against neoliberal interests and that is why I argue that the Left in India should take up the slogan of a

Socialist Knowledge Society, and project it as an alternative to neoliberalism.

An interesting debate is raging in the academic and business circles over the future role of intermediaries in a knowledge economy. While some argue that "disintermediation", or the elimination of intermediaries in the business processes of the future is a certainty, as e-commerce can eliminate the need for middlemen, some other school of thought puts forward the argument that instead of disintermediation, a counter phenomenon is occurring, that of "hypermediation" wherein in a netcentric economy, the number of middlemen will proliferate and the net instead of bringing the producer and consumer together, will actually put many more middlemen in between and all these players will get their share of the profit in any transaction depending on how advantageously they are placed in between. In fact both the processes, that is, "disintermediation" and "hypermediation" are not counter phenomena that are exclusive to each other, but are two sides of the same coin that form a vital aspect of e-commerce.

The Left has to popularise the concept of a "Socialist Knowledge Economy", whose broad characteristics I propose below.

1. Information Technology, like all other technologies is a double-edged sword. It can be used to intensify exploitation and dis-empower the vast majority while enriching a few individuals. In a socialist knowledge economy, the same IT can be used as a tool to bring about social and economic justice and prosperity for everybody. It is entirely at the discretion of those in power to choose, which way they have to wield the sword and to serve the class interests they choose to serve.

2. Our emphasis on IT initiative has to shift from cheap contract work for export to the development of high quality inward looking software and IT services that are specifically designed for India's development needs. The central and state governments should spare their resources in setting up high-end research centres to conduct core research in computer software, industrial process automation, bio-informatics, virtual reality and multimedia applications, geographical information systems, e-governance facilities, etc., which can be used for our own needs, without depending on outside MNCs. With a huge pool of IT and scientific experts, it is not an insurmountable task, provided we have the political will to execute.
3. In the case of bio-technology, India produces many bio-tech specialists, but a majority of them are jobless. Foreign MNCs use Indian expertise and experiment on Indian farmers. With a vast variety of crops, irrigation and environmental conditions, which differ from district to district, the need to develop new varieties of crops to suit local conditions is imperative. We can gainfully employ our bio-technology specialists to do research locally and develop genetically modified crops that suit our needs, without endangering the environment and safeguard bio-diversity. There is no limit to the degree of penetration of bio-technology into our agricultural sector and the consequent benefits it showers on our economy. We do not need multinationals to do this for us. The cost of setting up bio-technology lab facilities as well as the software for conducting research is coming down sharply, enabling smaller firms to enter this field, which till now is the sole domain of large MNCs. The core genetic research can be conducted by central and

state level labouratories. Thus a three-tier approach will be most effective.

4. The handloom sector in India is in ruins. Successive state governments and the neoliberal policies of the central government have virtually killed the handloom cooperatives. This condition can be reversed and we can bring back light into their lives by using advances in IT. Our young engineers can be entrusted with the task of manufacturing and maintaining computerised automatic weaving machines, which can be supplied to our weaving communities at affordable cost. Power looms should be allowed only in cooperatives. Weavers cooperatives can help the weavers' families to add more value by producing ready made garments and help market them. We have before us the experience of the Benetton Co-operative in Italy (The popular 'United Colours of Benetton' brand). Such a project is entirely viable and necessary. Besides improving the lot of the weavers, it will gainfully employ many engineers and computer specialists locally.
5. We can draw on the experience of innovative projects such as Canada's Newfoundland Knowledge Hub Project, where locally available IT expertise is integrated into the local economies to develop local resources such as agriculture, fisheries, food processing, traffic management, community health, tax collection, etc. Vast amounts of satellite data can be used by local expertise to develop geological information systems and maps that can be employed for water conservation and irrigation systems, flood and drought management, desalination and fresh water supply systems, non-conventional energy sources, micro-hydel power plants, roads, rural administration, etc. that will enrich local economies.

We can draw on the experience of China in developing micro-hydel power plants that can be run by local communities. Distributed power generation using locally available resources and managed locally is increasingly being seen as a more effective and environmentally friendly alternative.

6. The inter-linking of water bodies and water management and conservation should be taken up in a bottoms-up approach, with the task of building and maintaining irrigation and water conservation projects entrusted to local bodies. By bringing about more area of waste land to use, we can distribute land to the landless poor, help them to set up agricultural cooperatives that provide a safety net against adverse weather conditions and consequent crop failures, distribute fertilisers, pesticides and agricultural machinery and market their products. Local educated talent will have enormous opportunities in running such ventures. Agricultural reforms will be meaningful only when aided by such measures.

Much water has flown under the bridge. It is neither feasible nor is it correct to propose a centralised planned economy in this age of information. It is now possible, with the help of IT to build a decentralised planned socialist economy that can effectively function in a democratic environment, by empowering local governance. Developing localised centres of excellence by unleashing local talent should be the goal of the socialist knowledge economy, while eliminating exploitation and social and economic injustice. To paraphrase Lenin's statement, in today's context, socialist knowledge economy is local governance plus deployment of IT for empowering the masses.

3

Research in Human Health and Relevance of Dialectics

Soma Marla

A few days ago there was a report in the news media reporting the discovery of genes that could halt ageing and possibly extend human life ten times, i.e. well up to 800 years. Revolutionary developments we witness today in medicine, information technology and communications are fast changing the face of labour and are capable of influencing relations in society. It is in this context whether Marxism as a scientific method holds good for analysing science as a whole and its impact on society as a whole. Then there are others who argue that Marxism should limit itself to analysis of developments in economics and society and better keep off from science. Marxism is not merely a philosophy for analysis and interpretation of economy, human society and its transformation but also a valid scientific method that helps in understanding nature.

In spite of the axiomatic zigzag path traversed by it and the resulting amazing and sometimes complicated discoveries, Marxism sees science as an organ with an important social function. After all the very purpose of science is improvement of our knowledge about understanding nature and apply it for human betterment. The everyday changes witnessed today and the incremental changes brought about in productive forces in wealth production can be well examined by Marxist methods. After all Marxism uses its dialectical methods for analysis of various developments in science and their impact on society. It is possible to establish the regularities with which various scientific laws are working resulting in phenomena and novel products with enormous capability to increase production and thereby increase wealth and altering relations between different groups in our society.

Science can never be practised in isolation, but continues to move forward by discovering new phenomena defining existing regularities of changes in existing matter. The current understanding on behaviour of genes is arrived by scientific experimentation aided by accumulated earlier knowledge. Let us go back to the ageing problem we started our discussion with. Ageing of our body is controlled by hundreds of genes from the cell cycle whose behaviour defines health and development as we age. This particular discovery is nothing but a result of a sequence of historical experiments conducted through the last two centuries on structure and discovery of various cell division genes regulating various steps and development of our body. Firstly the genes operate in time and space, i.e. Genotype (very information inherited from parents that is written our genes) under the influence of environment. The environment in turn is intrinsically linked to nutrition, disease infections and in short in the web of socio-economic conditions the individual is subjected to live. In short, in Marxist understanding life is a special form of movement of matter that operates in time and space reflecting concreteness and flexibility. For example, a disease such as tuberculosis can be examined by inferring the structure of a human gene, its upstream located transcription factors that are heavily influenced by environmental factors such as nutrition, abundance of infection, etc. that regulate the expression and expression of the disease genes in our body.

This in turn depends on societal conditions under which one lives and the web of social and economic relations a diseased individual is subjected to. A scientific discovery resulting from experimentation is nothing but a necessary negation of the existing knowledge and updating it with new data demonstrating new phenomena that regulate motion in a new form. The new discovery brings in a totally new and qualitative change in understanding the problem under scientific investigation. Let us examine these scientific discoveries in context of the Hegelian concept of hierarchical classification of matter which is nothing but a mere blind journey from simplicity to complexity but also a successive increase of knowledge forms wrapping up one layer up on another, with its unique type of behaviour. Later Hegel's hierarchical classification was enriched by Marx by making every change dynamic that operates in time and space in context of evolution and formation of different species. Similarly no scientific investigation operates in isolation but requires a network of other disciplines in science for its logical experimentation. For example, take human tissue proteins infected with tuberculosis. Precise understanding of arrangement of different atoms in a protein molecule and design of drugs that are targeted to them will only be possible again by application of Physics to Biology.

Often it is noticed that in scientific papers experimental data are presented and conclusions are arrived at defending the experimenter's hypothesis. But seldom is it given why the investigator chose the problem to investigate (describing the pure scientific and social reasons) and how from the web of complex interactions he arrived at the conclusions. Also rarely discussed is how this invention (for example a new drug/vaccine) could influence society. In short, science never operates in isolation and must always be examined by application of various dialectical laws such as law of negation, transformation of quantity to quality, hierarchical classification which enables us to see the very purpose of practising science.

In a word, application of various Marxist methods of enquiry removes science from its imagined position of detachment from society and shows that it is a part of economic and social environment. This clearly demonstrates whom this sense of detachment and masking the social responsibility of modern science is benefiting in today's society. For example, it is very interesting to note that pharmaceutical MNCs are more interested in development of high profit earning cancer and anti-obesity drugs rather than malarial drugs for poorer sections of our population that are less profitable.

4

October Revolution

Facts and Fiction

Y.V. Krishna Rao

Introduction

We are living in the era of Scientific and Technological Revolution (STR) and Information and Communication Technology (ICT) which have brought rapid changes and transformations in the history of mankind. Knowledge and information are increasingly playing an important role in the present-day world. A deep study of these changes is very important and necessary to plan 21st century socialism. For this, a study of the successes and failures of the 20th century socialism will help us to redefine the meaning and contours of 21st century socialism.

This paper tires to capture a brief review of the October Revolution and its impact on world development. The first period of establishment of the Soviet State, Internal Civil War and external aggression of 14 capitalist, imperialist countries, New Economic Policy, rapid industrialisation, Second World War, defeat of fascism and Japanese military, 20th Party Soviet Congress, Gorbachev's Perestroika period, and collapse of the Soviet systems respectively have been covered.

The paper analyses the distortions in the Soviet economic, social and ideological fields. The paper ends with a new perspective of 21st century socialism.

Communists and progressives all over the world have commemorated the 90th anniversary of the Russian Revolution which marked the turning point in the history of the working class in meetings and ceremonies. In the socialist countries of Asia, on the Island of Cuba, in Eastern Europe and the former Soviet republics, communists paused from their work to recall the achievements of the Soviet Union that was born from the torch lit on November 7, 1917.

Though the Soviet Union is no more, the roar of the guns that triggered the popular uprising that swept the Bolsheviks to power echoes across the planet today. In People's China, Democratic Korea, Vietnam, Laos and Cuba the masses are taking their own roads to socialism, while throughout the Third World progressive forces have taken the socialist perspective to achieve liberation, independence and social justice in the world.

We remember the sacrifice of Soviet youth who smashed the Nazi legions in the Second World War and saved the world from fascism, democratic, progressive people of the world as, well as working people pay tribute to the immense Soviet contribution to the national liberation movements in breaking the chains of colonial slavery.

The 1917 October Revolution led to the establishment of the First Workers' and Peasants' state, the USSR, in 1922 and throughout much of its existence the Soviet Union was the hope of working people across the world. The colossal achievements of the Soviet Union, led by Lenin and Stalin, were living proof of the validity of the socialist system.

The October Revolution is the greatest event in the whole history of mankind and, like a greatest earthquake shook the capitalist world to its foundations. For the first time, humanity takes control over its destiny.

"There was no greater event during the 20th century than the October Revolution and it has affected all of human history," said Zyuganov Secretary General of the Communist Party of the Russian Federation on November 7 at the open rally in Moscow.

The shock of the October Revolution and the formation of the Soviet State had an immediate reflection on the movement against colonialism.The October Revolution created conditions for the extended rights, to the working people, even in non-developed capitalist countries.

After their direct military intervention failed and they have been forced to withdraw their military forces, the imperialists have realised that they cannot destroy the Soviet power by direct methods. Hence, they have changed their strategy to destroy the Soviet power, by indirect methods (i.e.) by helping the internal anti-Soviet force and also by planting their agents both in the government and the party. This they did successfully as the later events proved.

The gains of the workers and farmers under Soviet power functioned in favour of the working people in the capitalist countries. They were a basic factor that obliged the bourgeois governmental parties, liberals and social democrats to make concessions to the working class.

The shock of the October Revolution to the foundations of the old world order had an immediate positive reflection in the movements against colonialism.

The efforts of the young Soviet government to build the economic foundations of socialism advanced under the conditions of a hard struggle against the forces of foreign military intervention and the domestic bourgeoisie and Tsarists, imperialist encirclement and internal subversion, with conspiracies, sabotage and assassinations of communist cadres. The socialist revolution released the immense humane forces that not only managed to transform the former Russian empire building the economic foundations of socialism, but also developed the strengths necessary to become a great economic and military power by the eve of the imperialist Second World War. Thanks to the wisdom of the leadership of that time, the leadership of the Communist Party and the Soviet Union and the enormous effort, sacrifice and suffering of the Red Army and the Soviet people, socialism was secured and fascism was crushed.

For 40 years more, USSR develops and a Socialist World system came to existence and the national liberation movements brought down colonial and neo-colonial governments in Asia and Africa, and in Latin America, the Cuban revolution is victorious. The help and support from the first land of the worker and working-farmers the Soviet Union is essential in this transformation of the world and liberation of the people. As the October Revolution and the development of the Soviet Union and socialism was the greatest event in the history of the working class and the working people, the downfall of USSR and the socialist world system is our biggest setback ever.

Impact on World Development

The Bolsheviks' slogan in 1917 was *"Bread, land and peace"*.

The 1917 October Revolution led to the establishment of the first workers' and peasants' state, the USSR in 1922 and throughout much of its existence the Soviet Union was the hope of working people across the world. The colossal achievement of the Soviet Union, led by Lenin and Stalin, was living proof of the validity of the socialist system.

The Bolsheviks swept out the capitalists and land-owners and unleashed the immense potential of the workers and peasants to build a new life for themselves.

The oppressed nations of the Czarist Empire were freed and lived as equals in a Union of Soviet Socialist

Republics which guaranteed everyone work, education, science and culture. The socialist system created new men and women who rebuilt the country after the destruction of the Civil War, who struggled to create the industries needed for the future, who sacrificed themselves by the millions to defend the Soviet Union and defeat fascism in the Second World War.

While the economies of the imperialist world crashed, the people of the Soviet Union saw their living standards rise twelvefold. While the imperialists prepared for another world war, against themselves and eventually against the USSR, the Soviet Union worked tirelessly for collective security and peace.

While the imperialists mercilessly plundered Africa and Asia, the Soviet Union helped the world communist cause and the national liberation movement.

The October Revolution proved that working people could overthrow their oppressors and build their own state. Soviet power defeated the reactionary White Guards and the imperialist intervention led by Britain, France, Poland and Japan during the Civil War.

Soviet success destroyed the myths of the class-collaborationist social-democrats and Trotskyists.

Soviet power proved that it was possible to build socialism in one state. Soviet power smashed Nazi Germany and brought the Japanese Empire to its knees ending the Second World War in 1945.

Soviet democracy builds a new life for the working people of the USSR. Bourgeois democracy, which is essentially the dictatorship of the bourgeoisie, is based on the principle of the smallest number of people manipulating the largest number of votes. Soviet democracy showed that under the dictatorship of the proletariat genuine, popular, mass democracy would thrive. Soviet democracy inspired the people's democracies led by the communist and workers' parties of eastern Europe liberated in the Second World War and those leading the liberation struggle of the Chinese, Cuban, Korean and Southeast Asian peoples.

In 1871, the Paris Commune lit the torch that would blaze in October 1917 and those flames still burn in Asia and Latin America and in the communist movement throughout the world. And just as Marx, Engels and Lenin learnt from the experiences and defeat of the Commune we too can learn from the positive and negative experience of the Soviet Union.

The Soviet victory over the White Guards and the interventionist forces taught the imperialists a bitter lesson. They learned that Soviet power was most unlikely to be overthrown by direct offensive. They saw that their best hope was to undermine the revolution from within using elements of the former oppressive classes in the former Russian Empire and their agents within the Communist party to serve their purpose while mobilising social-democratic, revisionist, Trotskyist, fascist and reactionary religious elements inside and outside the USSR to mount an ideological offensive to isolate the new Soviet state and create the conditions for its downfall.

Stalin said in his speech at the Plenum of the Central Committee of the Communist Party of the Soviet Union in March 1937 that the class struggle would inevitably sharpen as the Soviet Union advanced towards socialism. He said: "We must smash and cast aside the rotten theory that with every advance we make the class struggle here must subside, the more successes we achieve the tamer will the class enemy become. This is not only a rotten theory but a dangerous one, for it lulls our people, leads them into a trap, and enables the class enemy to recuperate for the struggle against the Soviet Government. On the contrary, the further forward we advance, the greater the success we achieve, the greater will be the fury of the remnants of the defeated exploiting classes, the more prepared will they be to resort to sharper forms of class struggle, the more they will seek to harm the Soviet state, and the more will they clutch at the most desperate means of struggle as the last resort of the doomed."

Later revisionists would denounce this as another of Stalin's theoretical "mistakes" and argued the precise opposite. But what Stalin said was essentially what Lenin wrote: "Our revolution, more than any other, confirms the law that the impact of the revolution, the force of the offensive, the energy, decisiveness and triumph of its victory intensify the force of resistance by the bourgeoisie."

After the counter-revolutions in the Soviet Union and Eastern Europe in 1989 and 1990, can any genuine communist now argue that Lenin and Stalin were wrong?

When the counter-revolutionaries who had wormed their way to the top of the Soviet leadership destroyed the USSR, the imperialists rejoiced and told us that communism was finished. They said Marx and Engels were wrong. Their paid scribes claimed that "history was dead" and that from now on and forever more the entire planet would be governed by the exploiters. Their intellectual lackeys told us to expect a new era of common prosperity funded by a "peace dividend" with the end of the cold war and a "new world order" that would solve the problems of the planet.

What we got was imperialist wars for resources and land and an anti-working class offensive aimed at stripping working people of the gains won through struggle during the last century.

'Premature' Revolution

It has once again become fashionable to argue that the

Russian Revolution was premature that the economic conditions in backward Russia could not support the attempt to build a socialist society. This is the gist of Eric Hobsbawm, a well known Marxist historian and Karl Kautsky, German Social Democratic leader and Robin Blackburn, Editor, *New Left Review* and others.

Some have argued that the Russian Revolution was not a genuine people's revolution but a coup engineered by Lenin. But all these arguments were incorrect and baseless.

"Without the direct state support of the European proletariat the working class of Russia cannot remain in power and convert its temporary domination into a lasting socialistic dictatorship. Of this there cannot be any doubt. But on the other hand, there cannot be any doubt that a socialist revolution in the West will enable the Soviets to directly convert the temporary domination of the working class into a socialist dictatorship."

In the course of 1917, Lenin and the Bolsheviks adopted this perspective wholeheartedly Even Stalin could summarise the differences between Lenin, on the one hand, and Zinoviev and Kamenev, on the other, over whether to make the October Revolution in these terms: "There are two lines; one sets the course for the victory of the revolution and relies on Europe, the second does not believe in the revolution and counts only on being an opposition."

And Lenin, in an oft-repeated argument, said: "It is not open to the slightest doubt that the final victory of our revolution if it were to remain alone, if there were no revolutionary movement in other countries, would be hopeless... Our salvation from all these difficulties, I repeat, is an all European revolution."

These were not, as Robin Blackburn claims, "Lenin and Trotsky's later justifications of the original Bolshevik seizure of power." They were the avowed perspective of the Bolsheviks before, during and after the October Revolution. And the Bosheviks were not alone in hoping for a European revolution. Even Kautsky, in a passage from 1904 which somehow seems to escape the notice of his modern admirers, acknowledged the possibility of a revolution in Germany which must lead to the political domination of the proletariat in Western Europe and create for the Eastern European proletariat the possibility of contracting the stages of their development and copying the example of the Germans, artificially setting up socialist institutions.

Kautsky could not quite shake off the power of the Bolsheviks' analysis state that: The Bolsheviks must not be blamed too much for expecting a European revolution. Other socialists did the same, and we are certainly approaching conditions which will sharply accentuate the class struggle, and which may have many surprises in store.

In the post-war years, the Bolsheviks' prognosis was proved absolutely correct. There was a European-wide revolutionary upheaval. The Easter Rising in Ireland pre-dated the October Revolution. The fall of the German Kaiser, precipitated by a naval mutiny and a general strike, followed the revolution in November 1918. More revolutionary crises ensued.

In March 1919 a Soviet government assumed power in Hungary and in the same year a massive labour unrest shook the British state to its foundations. For the two red years, Italy was convulsed by massive class struggles.

The newspapers of the period covered the reverses in Western Europe as astonishing... riots in Paris, riots in Lyon, revolution in Belgium, revolution in Constantinople, victory of the Soviets in Bulgaria, rioting in Copenhagen. In fact the whole of Europe is in movement, clandestine or open Soviets and appearing everywhere, evening the Allied armies, everything is possible, everything."

At the other end of the political spectrum, Lloyd George wrote: "The whole of Europe is filled with the spirit of revolution. There is a deep sense not only of discontent but of anger revolt amongst the workmen against the pre-war conditions. The whole existing order in its political, social and economic aspects is questioned by the masses of the population from one end of Europe to the other."

The Bolsheviks correctly predicted a European revolution and they trained their might and main to provide the revolution with a leadership which could bring it to a successful conclusion. The war against the interventionary forces resulted in vast destruction of the country's economy. Scarcity of everything needed to safeguard life. There were food riots in several places. So Lenin gave up economics where communism put in its place a new economic plan of mixed economy. To change the economy from war communism to new economic planning (NEP) of mixed economy is not an easy thing. There was stiff opposition from the party and the war king class. Lenin had to struggle a great deal to convince the Party of the necessity and urgency to adopt the new economy.

He also said "we don't know how long this period of new economy may last." After Lenin's death, Stalin changed Lenin's path of Soviet development. He changed the NEP Policy and carried out forced collectivisation of private farms. By 1930, Stalin's authoritarian dictatorial repressive rule was established. He eliminated all the old guard.

Elimination of All Old Genuine Revolutionaries by Stalin

Lenin scrupulously tried to safeguard the party's internal democratic functioning, even in the most critical times and allowed discussions on all major events and also to safeguard state democratic functioning. Stalin, on the other hand, put a stop to the democratic functioning both in the party and state and stamped every difference as inimical, thus eliminating the revolution of the old guard. He established his personal dictatorship over the party as well as the state and let loose a repressive rule and terror in the Soviet Union.

Planning was drawn centrally and executed, with the help of the bureaucracy. There was no participation of the people at large either in the shaping of the plan as well its execution. Thus, the whole planning was over centralised and bureaucratic. The ideological education of the working people and also the development of ideology according to the changing conditions were completely given up.

The 20th Soviet Party Congress and Khrushchev's Wrong Propositions

Even after Beria's episode, the Soviet party under Khrushchev's leadership had not drawn correct lessons that the imperialists were trying day in and day out to destroy socialism in the Soviets and elsewhere. There was no let up in their efforts ever since the days of the 14 capitalist imperialist countries intervention in 1918.

We can see the bitter fight that went on in Latin America between the forces struggling for building democratic socialism in their countries and between the forces of anti-socialists, capitalist imperialist forces, led by America. The imperialist forces were able to defeat the recent national referendum in Venezuela on changes in the constitution that allowed some radical changes further to build socialism. The 20th Soviet Party Congress held in 1956, analysis of the Soviet economy and the American and world economy was completely wrong.

The 20th Party Congress' theoretical and political propositions of peaceful coexistence, peaceful revolutions, etc., were entirely wrong. The imperialists proposed their counter proposals (See Appendix No. 1 Economic and Political Journal's extract). These details can be found in Appendix 1. How can there be peaceful existence between two rival social systems, each of which was trying to destroy the other? The other proposition of the 20th Party Congress was that the Soviet communists had become a party of the whole people. This is also a wrong formulation. The sum and substance of the 20th Party Congress formulations were not only wrong in several aspects but it also blunted the vigilance against the country's revolutionary activities of imperialists. It was a completely wrong overestimation of the Soviet economy and gross underestimation of the American economy. With this wrong understanding, Khrushchev boasted that the Soviet economy would overtake the American economy in a short time. This overestimation of the Soviet economy and under-estimation of the American economy also continued in the 1957 and 1961 documents of the World Communist Parties' meetings held in Moscow.

The vigilance against the imperialists' penetration of the Soviet state and party was almost given up. This situation was fully used by those anti-socialist forces to penetrate into the Soviet Party and the state and these forces later on worked for the collapse of the socialist countries of Central and Eastern Europe in 1989 and the Soviet Union in 1991. Khrushchev's so-called secret report on Stalin's criminal actions resulted in demoralising the Soviet people.

Accelerated Industrialisation

The period of accelerated industrialisation since 1930 was the most important period in strengthening the Soviet economy to face the coming Second World War. With the rise of Nazism in Germany, Fascism in Italy and Manchuria by Japan war lords were thickening. So the Soviet Union also had to strengthen its military and economic foundations. It was a period of impressive, incomparable and impossible to repeat development, and was also a period of the Soviet people's total mobilisation.

On the other hand, it was a period of intense internal and external fights. It was during this period that the Soviet government took the characteristics known nowadays, with its magnitudes and miseries. The urgency of the inexperience and the theoretical and practical mistakes were the factors in the rapid construction of communism. The need for an ultra centralised command in order to even ensure the total mobilisation to face the enemies' sabotages and threats resulted in a debilitation of the socialist democracy, class democracy and popular democracy. The essence of proletariat directorship was perverted. The economic system did not satisfactorily solve the antinomy between the intensive and extensive development, which created negative repercussion in the provision of the popular classes goods and services.

The Great Electrification Plan of Russia (GOELRO Plan) ensured the power supplies to all areas in the country, thus having a profound affect on daily life and industrial production. Modern industrial sectors, which had not existed under the feudal regime, were established in a short period. Russia was able to produce all the necessary goods for national development and progress and for defence against foreign aggressors. Several years after the war, Soviet power lifted the country out of devastation. An anti-nuclear weapons shield, nuclear power plants and nuclear-powered ice breakers for peaceful purposes were built. Only 12 years after the devastating war, the Soviet Union launched the world's first man-made satellite into space, ushering in the possibility of sending a man into space. Other notable records included free health care and education, house building on a large scale, stable prices, high development of knowledge and healthy social relations and morality, creating a foundation for ensuring a high quality population and strong belief in the future and younger generations. Nationalities in the Soviet Union lived and supported each other. Millions of marriages were held among different nationalities. Cultural and traditional values were carefully preserved.

Each period of the socialist construction has had its historical importance. Each one has created the circumstances which, beyond good and evil, have given the raw material to the new society magnificence and miseries.

Gorbachev's Glasnost and Perestroika

By the time Gorbachev became the General Secretary of the Party and President of the Soviet State the country's internal situation was in a crisis. The party's command on the people was at zero point. Workers' strikes were on the increase. Minority nationalities were up against Russian domination.

Gorbachev had not properly understood the situation. Without first correcting the situation in the party and without making any effort to unite the party, Gorbachev tried to follow his plan of action. With this the internal situation further worsened leading finally to the collapse of the system itself.

From all the distortions, wrong estimates of the economy and wrong proposition of the 20th Party Congress, proper lessons were due to be taken.

Was this inevitable? Nothing is inevitable. If the institutional basis for more developed socialism and the cleansing power of glasnost had emerged earlier; if the leadership had been different, if say, Gorbachev had come along ten years earlier at a time when the reservoir of patriotic support and popular mandate was still strong; and if the world's working-class movement had been stronger, then the negative deformations could have been overcome without the loss of Soviet state power and the horrendous suffering imposed on the post-Soviet peoples today. So the fall of the USSR had structural causes, but not in the sense that the socialist system or model was wrong. According to David Libman, Professor of Economics at the City University of New York and Editor of *Science and Society* the blame lies with the structural aspects of the political and cultural deformation. Many people blame Gorbachev, saying that he "sold out". But David Libman thinks this is superficial. According to him, Gorbachev had to walk a knife-edge. On one side you had the entrenched bureaucratic system, and on the other, you had political chaos. It would have taken a politician larger than life to survive that. To blame Gorbachev, or "human error", misses the point.

Socialism, Objective Need

The cycle opened in 1917 was blocked by the socialism degeneracy and interrupted by the failure of the first experiences of the construction of socialism, a historical failure which has created a new world situation and produced an important change in the correlation between the progressive and conservatives forces.

According to Zyuganov Secretary General, the Communist Party of Russian Federation, the strength and potential of the Soviet State based on the October Revolution, helped maintain world peace and controlled the imperialists' ambitions, preventing imperialism from setting up a regime based on bombs and shells. ("The anti-communist forces in Russia and in the world are finding ways and means to hide the fact that socialist ideologies have had a very positive influence of the fate of many nations which only half a century ago were still colonies"). He further stressed that: "The achievements of China are not only undeniable but also indispensable. It is the Communist Party which is the force that has led China to become one of the leading countries in the world. The Socialist Republic of Vietnam gained great achievements. Laos has also seen positive changes. Communists worldwide, first of all in Asia, have found new and effective forms of socialist construction.

This is a bright example in creativity and a proof that parties operating in different conditions can work together to enrich the theory and practice of socialist construction. Forty per cent of the world population is living in the countries with communist parties as the leaders to participants in the management of the state. This means that nearly half of humanity volunteers to follow socialism. This is a forceful evidence today of the vitality of the basis of the October Revolution. It is clear that socialism is not the past, but the future of humanity."

Distortions in the Soviet Model of Socialism

Looking back we can see that the historic achievements of the Soviet Union in the early decades in the face of enormous difficulties which had blurred the reality that the transition to socialism is a protracted and complex process. Lenin had warned at the outset itself saying that, "We have only just taken the first steps towards shaking off capitalism altogether and beginning the transition to socialism. We do not know and we cannot know how many stages of transition to socialism there will be." (Gol. *Works*, Vol. 27, p. 31) Further Lenin had stated, "The more backward the country, which, owing to the zigzags of history has proved to be the one to start the socialist revolution, the more is it difficult for that country to pass from its old capitalist relations to socialist relations". (Vol. 27, p. 89) It must be recognised that a weakness of Marxist theory has been the under development of the creative thought in the study of existing socialism and the development of a new society as compared to its strong and comprehensive analysis of the capitalist system. Without going into a detailed enquiry into the causes for the dismantling of the Soviet Union, the lessons from it have to be grasped so that a coherent Marxist-Leninist understanding provides the ground work for future progress.

According to Prakash Karat, General Secretary, CPI (M), to enrich Marxist-Leninist theory and practice some of the salient features which require critical study are:

1. Socialist democracy: The institutionalisation of democratic forums and participation of people in the political process and economic management;
2. Need for a correct relationship between the state and the party in a socialist society.
3. Flexibility in the management of the economy and multiplicity of the forms of ownership of property at different stages.

To build socialism in a world where capitalism remains dominant of substantial strength, requires a theoretical perspective which recognises the paramount lesson that the transition to socialism and the building of socialism, particularly in less developed capitalist countries is a more protracted and complex process than it was envisaged under the impact of the October Revolution. The substantial and historic achievements of socialism in the Soviet Union should be drawn upon to develop the theoretical basis for seeing the entire period of achieving the socialist revolution and building socialism as a diverse process where there can be no one model. Socialism will be built in a country in a context where capitalist relations and influences will continue to prevail for a long period of time both internationally and domestically. In such a situation the difficult task of building an alternative model of socialist development will require constant raising and rejuvenation of political consciousness by the active participation of the people at all stages of political and economic development. It is here that the vital importance of socialist democracy is located. The sobering and hard lesson for the future is that the absence of democracy in any socialist experiment, the failure to expand and develop the potential of democracy will deform and distort socialism.

He further says this requires giving up the entrenched notion of public ownership being equated with only state ownership. Different forms of public ownership, other than State ownership, are necessary to prevent bureaucraticism and stagnation. The coexistence of planned and commodity market sectors will have to be constantly updated and innovated. Central planning as a singular/ centralised model must give way to plans at different levels and the vital element of popular participation. The coexistence with capitalist forms necessitates the continuous ideological struggle against the bourgeois ideology it engenders and its corrupting influences. This is possible only if the revolutionary party does not confine its role to administering the state and managing the economy. The parties in the Soviet Union and East Europe played no role as independent agencies for waging an ideological struggle and political work among the people. This in turn is related to the lack of institutionalising socialist democracy which is not possible by merging the ideology of the party with the state. ("Reality of Imperialism and the Future of Socialism" by Prakash Karat, paper presented to the International Workshop held at Havana, October, 21–23, 1997).

Development of Human Forces

Thus, building the new society stresses not the growing

production of things but, rather, creation of the conditions for development of human forces—i.e. conditions which replace capitalism's fragmented, crippled human beings with the totally developed individual and permit people to develop through their own activity. With the 'all-round' development of the individual all the springs of cooperative wealth would flow more abundantly. This concept of socialism for the 21st century rescues Marx's original idea of an 'association, in which the free development of each is the condition for the free development of all', a society focused on the development of all human powers as such the end in itself. It embraces Che Guevara's stress in his classic work, *Man and Socialism in Cuba,* that in order to build socialism it is essential, along with building new material foundations, to build new human beings. Thus, it rejects the practice of ignoring the transformation of social relations and human beings in order to develop productive forces—an unfortunate characteristic of the top-down efforts at building socialism in the 20th century.

On Socialisation of the Means of Production

One question is, "What is a socialist economy?" The JCP Programme defines that a socialist economy is characterised by the "socialisation of the means of production". Let me explain more about this definition. In the capitalist economy, factories and machines, which are the means of production, are operated collectively by workers, who serve the entire society and the people. In that sense, although the means of production has already taken on a social character, it is not under social ownership, but owned by individual capitalists who are motivated to run factories and the economy by the quest of larger profits, not by the desire to serve the public interests. We call it a profit-first principle, which lies at the root of various contradictions inherent in capitalist society. The socialisation of the means of production is there to solve these contradictions. The factories and machines, that is, the means of production, which are in effect operated collectively by workers throughout society, must come under social ownership. This concept is aimed at promoting the rational development of the economic system of the society and constitutes the essence of socialism. If so, then, what does social ownership of the means, of production really mean? This in fact is a major question. In the Soviet Union, "Nationalisation" establishing state ownership of factories and machines was considered as the "socialisation of the means of production" in a socialist economy. Is "nationalisation" of the means of production sufficient to realise socialism? In my view, this represents the misconception that caused the. failure of the Soviet Union because it built a society that had nothing in common with socialism in spite of its claim to being a socialist country.

Marx was not such a simple-minded person that he would argue that a transfer of control over the means of production to the state through nationalisation will achieve socialism. In *Capital*, Marx argued extensively about socialism and communism. He repeatedly emphasised that the social ownership of the means of production is essential in socialism and communism. But nowhere in *Capital* did he explain that "socialism" means state ownership of the means of production. Who did Marx say holds the means of production? He said "associated workers" do. I said that even under capitalism, workers form groups to operate the means of production instead of doing work individually in large-scale industries using machinery. In other words, "associated workers" actually run factories. These associated workers are the key players in productive activities, but they are not treated as the main players in the economy. The need is to change it to make these "associated workers" have a grip on the means of production as the key players of productive activities in the real sense of the word.

This was precisely what Marx characterised socialism as "socialisation of the means of production". In *Capital,* Marx also describes the socialist or communist economy as the associated mode of production, because the associated producers hold in their hands the means of production. Nationalisation could be an important step as) a concrete form of "socialisation of the means of production", but there can be a variety of other forms. In future historical developments, the "socialisation of the means of production" can be realised in a form other than nationalisation. Whatever the forms may be, the principal standard for identifying a form as socialist must be whether "associated workers" are playing the main role or not. If bureaucrats keep everything under their control and repress workers, the key players of production, in the name of "socialisation of the means of production" and "socialism" such a system cannot be called socialism. If you think more about it, you will be able to grasp the features of socialism. (Lecture by Tetsuzo Fuwa, Chair, Japanese Communist Party at the 38th Akahata Festival Tokyo, November 3, 2007).

We will conclude this paper by quoting the concluding section of the talk by Michael Lebowitz on "Socialism Does Not Drop from the Sky", Venezuela on July 24, 2005 which elaborates the Bolivarian constitution of Venezuela in which the distortions of 20th century soviet socialism were corrected ad new features of 21st century socialism were briefly defined.

We need to understand that socialism of the 21st century cannot be a statistic society where decisions are top-down and where all initiative is the property of state office-holders or cadres of self-reproducing vanguards. Precisely because socialism focuses on human development, it stresses the need for a society which is democratic, participatory, and protagonistic. A society dominated by an all-powerful state does not produce the human beings who can create socialism. For the same reason, socialism is not populism. A society in which people look towards the state to provide them with resources and with the answers to all their problems does not foster the development of human capacities; rather, it leaves, them as people who look to the state for all answers and to leaders who promise everything. Further, socialism is not totalitarianism. Precisely because human beings differ and have differing needs and abilities, their development by definition requires recognition and respect for diversity. Neither state nor community pressures for uniformity in productive activity, consumption choices, or lifestyles support the emergence of what Marx welcomes as unity based upon recognition of difference. We need to recognise, too, that socialism is not the worship of technology—a disease that has plagued Marxism and which in the Soviet Union took the form of immense factories, mines, and collective farms to capture presumed economics of scale. Rather, we must acknowledge that small enterprises may both permit greater democratic control from below (thus developing the capacities of the producers) and also may better preserve an environment which can serve the needs of people. We can learn the lessons from the experiences of the 20th century. We know now that the desire to develop a good society for people is not sufficient—you have to be prepared to break with the logic of capital in order to build a better world. And we know that socialism cannot be achieved from above through the efforts and tutelage of a vanguard which seises all initiatives and distrusts the self-development of the masses. "The working class, "Rosa Luxemburg wisely stressed, "demands the right to make its own mistakes and learn in the dialectic of history". When we begin from the goal of a society which can unleash all the potential of human beings and recognise that the path to that goal is inseparable from the self-development of people, we can build a truly human society.

I suggest, in fact, that many lessons of the 20th century have been learned and are embodied in the Bolivarian Constitution. In Article 299's emphasis on "ensuring overall human development", in the declaration of Article 20 that "everyone has the right to the free development of his or her own personality" in the focus of Article 102 on "developing the creative potential of every human being and the full exercise of his or her personality in a democratic society," in Article 62's declaration that participation by people is "the necessary way of achieving the involvement to ensure their complete development, both individual and collective", in the identification of democratic planning and participatory budgeting at all levels of society and the focus in Article 70 upon "self-management, co-management, cooperatives in all levels of society" and the focus in Article 70 upon "self-management, comanagement, cooperatives in all forms" as and in the obligations noted in Article 135 which, "by virtue of solidarity, social responsibility and humanitarian assistance, are incumbent upon private individuals according the their abilities"—the elements of a socialism of the 21st century are there in ideal form. The struggle now is to make them a reality.

There had been a distortion of Marxism both in theory and in practice—a distortion that forgot about human beings, a determinist message focusing on productive forces, I argued, could never understand why Marx sacrificed his "health, happiness and family" to write *Capital*. Nor could it make sense of why Marx never stopped stressing that workers could make themselves fit to create a new society only through the process of struggle.

The point was simple; as Che Guevara had stressed in his classic *Man and Socialism in Cuba,* to build socialism it is essential, along with building new material foundations, to build new human beings. But how? I focused on a number of elements. Self-management in the process of production, I argued, was an essential element: "Insofar as people produce themselves in the course of all their activities, the very process of engaging in democratic forms of production is an essential part of producing people for whom the need for cooperation is second nature." But self-management in particular productive units is not sufficient. You need, I argued, to replace a focus upon selfishness and self-orientation with a focus upon community and solidarity, a conscious emphasis upon human needs; i.e. the necessity to engage in collective solutions to satisfy human needs must be "recognised as a responsibility of all individuals" And, producing people with these characteristics could never be achieved by a state standing over and above civil society. "Rather, only through their own activities through autonomous organisations—at the neighbourhood, community and national levels—can people transform both circumstances and themselves". What, in short, was necessary was "the conscious development of a socialist civil society."

This, rather than a focus on the development of productive forces, I stressed the centrality of human beings and the development of the institutions which permit them to transform themselves. This had not occurred in the Soviet model. "With its lack of democratic and cooperative production, its absence of a socialist civil society and its actually existing bureaucratic rule", so-called real socialism had not produced the new human beings who could build a better world.

Social ownership of the means of production is critical because it is the only way to ensure that our communal, social productivity is directed to the free development of all rather than used to satisfy the private goals of capitalists, groups of individuals, or state bureaucrats. Social ownership, however, is not the same as state ownership. State property is consistent with state capitalist enterprises, hierarchical statistic firms, or firms in which particular groups of workers (rather than society as a whole) capture the major benefits of this state property. Social ownership implies a profound democracy—one in which people function as subjects, both as producers and as members of society. For sure, the socialism overthrow was not due to a spontaneous evolution. It was the result of a battle in which the imperialist enemies' pressure and their agents role in the society interior had considerable importance.

APPENDIX

50 Years Ago, *The Economic Weekly*, A Journal of Current Economic and Political Affairs, Vol. IX, No. 41, October 12, 1957

Moscow's Peace Offer

Gamblers and speculators may be unproductive members of society, but neither their capacity for intelligent anticipation nor their sense of realism has ever been in doubt. Wall street might have been cynical, but it was not unrealistic in boosting war equities on the assumption that the launching of an earth satellite by Russia seems to have correctly anticipated Washington's reaction to Moscow's scientific achievement Khrushchev's offer to ensure international control of all new scientific developments, including the earth satellite and all pilot less missiles, so as to avoid "the dangers of even more horrible weapons that science was bringing to the horizon" of an understanding between USA and USSR on peaceful coexistence has been promptly turned down on the plea that America is opposed to any bilateral agreement with Russia. Washington's rejection of Moscow's gesture is sought to be justified on the ground that any such bilateral agreement would be contrary to the principles of the Charter.

There is something in the argument, but it can be emphasised. It is an undeniable fact that there can be no world peace without a prior understanding between the two giants. More than once, similar offers by Russia have been rejected by America on the same grounds. America's concern for the prestige ad authority of the United Nations is commendable. But a closer analysis of the world situation makes it clear that reasons for the repeated rejection of Russia's appeal for an agreement on peaceful coexistence lie elsewhere. America and her Western allies may not be unwilling to reach an understanding with Russia. But they have insisted over and over again that the Soviet Union will have to accept their terms and conditions for an agreement on world peace. It is the Western Powers' obstinate refusal to agree to disagree that perpetuates 'cold war' and the resultant world tension.

Such an uncompromising attitude on so vital an issue as world peace can hardly ever have any logic behind it. It ceases to have the least justification after repeated peace offers by Russia. Ever since the "cold war", the Western Powers have seemed arrogant. It was these powers which pursued a policy of building positions of strength. Such a policy was defended on the ground that only thus could Russia be forced to negotiate on world peace.

5

India's Path to Socialism

Yugal J. Rayalu

1. Introduction

Sixty years after gaining independence the consolidation of power by the erstwhile rulers, land owners, the zamindars and the kulaks as the 'Respectable Ruling Political Class' gets a fillip as India prepares herself to integrate with world capitalism.

The accelerated rate of growth measured in terms of GDP and GNP is creating an Indian brand of Monopoly Capitalists, notwithstanding the fact that 20,000 farmers have committed suicide during the lást one decade. Never before in the history of India did the farmers, the real worshippers of Mother Earth, feel so frustrated and dejected by the apathy of the ruling class. Unfortunately the protest, if at all, is very feeble!

Opposition to the anti-worker and anti-farmer policies of the present government has only come from the left in general and from the communists in particular. Surprisingly almost everyone in the country acknowledges the role of the left in bringing the government's attention to the plight of the peasants and the workers. Staunch opponents of the leftists admit privately that the leftist movement has contributed immensely towards the upliftment of the marginalised sections of the society in India. Right sine the days of the First Parliament after Independence, the debates in Parliament have been directed by the left thinking, in support or against their agenda.

Yet the Communists have a very small presence in the national polity of India, at least in terms of representation in Parliament, legislative assemblies and local self-governing bodies. Naturally in spite of our intellectual strength, in spite of our continuous struggle we cannot hope to achieve a socialist pattern of governance with this strength. We cannot ensure that people's issues will get priority and prominence at the decision-making levels. Marx has said, "The Judiciary, the Executive and the Bureaucracy serve the interests of the class that rules over the society."

Being an important part of the independence struggle, it was very natural for the communists in India to have chosen the path of Parliamentary Democracy to establish socialism in India. In a country where 70% of the population lives the life of poverty and deprivation, where getting a square meal every day is a big challenge and where getting a regular job is a dream, what better could be the path? Parliamentary democracy has the potential to organise the working class without the use of violence. There may be hurdles in the path of working class becoming the ruling class, yet this is the path to achieve the goal of equality, justice and dignity. The majority has to decide the path of governance. Once this majority is motivated to fight for its own rights no one can stop them. The question is how to motivate this majority to assert its own rights.

2. Unity of the Working Class

In spite of the talk of the struggle by all the trade unions, the fact remains that only 6% of the total workforce in India is united in some way. The vast majority of the working class is unorganised and hence remains outside the gamut of any struggle for justice to the working class. The composition of the working class in India suffers a big drawback. We are divided by caste, religion and region. The ruling elite of the country has been using these divisive forces to keep the working class divided over the centuries. Many big Trade Union strikes have been broken by the use of caste and religious conflicts. The feudal-minded ruling class has not abandoned these tools in spite of our efforts to secularise the polity of the country.

It is very important that the working class gets united! And the task of achieving this unity lies with the leftists in general and with the communists in particular. The capitalist class is solidly united as far as fighting the class enemy (the leftists) is concerned. The need is for the deprived class to get united and build a society that addresses their problems. It is a fact that the majority of India is poor, yet the governments elected by these poor masses regularly take the anti-poor decisions. The reason behind this dichotomy is the disunity amongst the working class of our society. In spite of being in a majority this class is totally neglected and marginalised by the ruling feudal class of the country.

We need to work on two fronts. One is to make efforts to get a good representation in Parliament and the legislative bodies. The other is to make efforts to forge a broad unity of the working class. The beginning, as many may feel, has to come from the political parties. This may be true, yet there are alternatives. At the political level unity needs synchronisation of the ideologies, which is a gigantic task. The social composition of Indian society throws a big challenge before the left political leadership to unite this class. The Indian civil society appreciates the secular characteristic of the left in this country. Yet this is the very reason why the entire working class, including the peasantry gets carried away by the pseudo patriotic rhetoric of the capitalist class.

The working class has no hesitation in accepting the left political leadership as the vanguard as far as the struggle for justice is concerned. But the same class does not accept the same leadership when the question of electing the political representatives comes. It is a matter of serious discussion, why this dichotomy occurs.

Our experience in Kerala shows that a movement totally entwined with local social dynamics is highly successful. The left movement in Kerala goes far far beyond the political boundaries. Every aspect of social life is affected by the left movement and vice-versa.

One of the prerequisites for a broader unity is the cognizance of the local socio-political reality. Unfortunately we, the Communists in India, have in the past tried to define our socio-political situation in the light of the Western leftists. Secularism in the West has an altogether different connotation than what we have here. Similar is the truth about religion. We may be atheists because of our rational thinking. But let us not forget that the society at large is not atheist. The mother of a trade unionist may be a serious devotee of some deity or a follower of some cult. Do we demand total atheism from the family? How far would the party discipline go?

The fact is that the minorities in any society are very sensitive about their socio-cultural and religious identity. We cannot, and should not challenge that. Neither should we try to keep ourselves away from the reality of the religious sensitivity of the working class, at least till a socio-political consciousness is aroused in the working class towards class struggle.

Our concentration should be on the unity of the working class, not just for political reasons, but also as a matter of a long lasting relationship for a prolonged battle with the established capitalist class. Divisive factors like caste, religion and region should not be allowed to come in the way of the working class unity. Unfortunately today the working class is divided not only on political lines but also on the basis of region and castes.

Caste

Of late, the communists have started talking in terms of caste being a big problem in Indian society. Earlier they used to think that, once the economic problem is solved, the caste problem will automatically vanish. Unfortunately, the economic revolution has not occurred. The capitalist class finds it very suitable that the caste equation is kept alive as its arithmetic equation in the parliamentary election makes their manipulation very easy. The media unashamedly analyses the election results on the basis of caste, religion and region. We stand defeated. Our secularism stands defeated. The working class remains defeated. We cannot and should not ignore the caste equation, more so when the negative impact of caste is disastrous for the working class. The class struggle in India has to be inclusive of Dr. Ambedkar's thought. Not without it.

Religion

For a very long time we have ignored the power of religion in determining the social psyche. Most of the time religion has been used to divide the working class. The challenge is to use religion to unite the working class. It is true that many followers of religion desist from any call of class struggle, calling the pathetic situation of the poor people as the dictate of destiny. But it is also true that many religious persons in India today are using that very religion to unite people to fight for their rights. Swami Agnivesh has been relentlessly fighting against the draconian system of 'Bonded Labour'. The National Council of Churches in India has a separate cell to educate their congregation on the issues of labour. There is no reason why we should distance ourselves from such activities. In fact these institutions have no problem in seeking the help of 'Comrades' while dealing with the issues of labour. The only need for us is to be judicious in our approach.

There is no question about our approach about religious dogmatism and 'obscurantism'. As rationalists it is our duty to fight against all forms of dogma and blind faith. But then while doing this, we must not forget that, while fighting against these chains of mental slavery, our aim is to liberate the working class, not to indulge in any war of words with the religious institutions.

Trade Unions

At a rally in Nagpur, to protest against the anti-worker policies of the then central government, Com. Bardhan had called for a 'broad unity of the trade unions for the struggle against the onslaught of the forces of LPG'. It is true that in any particular industry, where the issues are common and a broad based understanding can be easily reached, it is pertinent to have a single union so that the sharpness of the struggle is strengthened so that the workers get the benefit of this unity. Decision-making becomes easy and negotiations are focused on the issues of justice to the workers. On many issues today there is a broad understanding amongst the left trade unions. This unity can be further consolidated to take the task of class struggle forward.

Unity of trade union across the different sectors should be the next step, to consolidate the philosophy of "Workers of all Sectors Unite!" Today many times workers of different sectors are at loggerheads when it comes to fight against the establishment. When the workers of a particular sector go on strike, it is very common to hear from the workers of other sectors complain that such strikes are making their life very difficult. They are more worried about their personal discomfort of a day, than to make any efforts to understand the real cause of the strike. The absence of "solidarity" makes the task of the fighting workers more difficult. As such the media controlled by the corporate houses is always in the forefront to criticise any and all strikes in the garb of 'Patriotism' and 'National Duty'.

3. Education

The motivation to fight against the anti-working class forces, comes, not just through sufferings, but also from education. Centuries old beliefs in destiny and religious blind faith are so strong that any amount of suffering is unable to create the urge to fight. It is the process of education that brings in the consciousness and the urge to know the real cause of suffering. The tools of Marxist education are very strong. The tragedy is that they are inadequately used. All over the world, history is understood with Marxian tools of understanding. All paleontologists use the tools of materialistic arguments to reach any understanding of the situation. The saffron brigade is most uncomfortable on this account because, their entire edifice is based on belief, not on any rationality. They consider the Marxian approach as the main enemy in their path to power. The traditionalists also consider Darwin as their enemy, because the theory of evolution has unmasked the lie about 'Man being sent by God from Heaven'. It must be a matter of pride for the Marxists that we are on the same side of the great scientists as far as understanding the world is concerned. Yet we are unable to realise the true potential of Marxian education.

Look at the pathetic condition of party education in different states today. Only a few select districts have regular party schools. Unfortunately many of our leaders are also apathetic to party schools for the reasons best known to them. Over the period of the last few years we have completely neglected the education aspect in our party. There are scores of party brethren who have joined the party long ago yet never had a chance to attend any party school. These loyal soldiers of the party are at a loss to understand the national and international developments. They are not equipped to face the onslaught of the media over the issues like the Singur/US-India Nuclear deal. Many of the party leaders went into deep hibernation at the time of the collapse of the Soviet Union, not because they were afraid of the situation but because they were unable to understand the dynamics of the situation then. Many trade union middle level leaders had started talking about the need to abandon the path of class struggle and accept the triumph of market over Marx. These were the Trade Union leaders who never went beyond the issue of 'bonus and pay rise' as far as understanding the class struggle is concerned.

It should be made compulsory for all party cadres to attend party school before they are given any posts or responsibilities. This should be done not as a matter of compulsion but as a matter of strengthening the cadre, to go forward.

Let us not forget that the tools of Marxian philosophy not only give us the direction, but also give us the strength to make our own views about the developments that we face. Without Marxian philosophical understanding there would be no difference between the cadre of our party and any saffron party. Both are very disciplined and highly motivated. The real and only difference is in our understanding of history and our path to the future. Our future is not political power. It is just a step towards our goal of creating an egalitarian society where all forms of exploitation are abolished. The major problem with our trade union cadre is that they are very narrowly focused on their internal issues. We have to make them to realise the importance of having a broader vision so that the march towards our ultimate goal is initiated at the earliest.

4. Socialism is the Future: Build it Now

Recently the South African Communist Party gave a slogan, "Socialism is the future, build it now!" We use the slogan "Socialism is the Future, Build it Now" to assert our deep conviction that socialism is the only just, rational and sustainable future for the people of our country and humanity at large; and that this future has to be struggled for here and now. Future does not begin in future. It begins now. Socialism is not the goal. Rather, the goal is the full development of human potential. Socialism is the path to that goal. It is only the path.

The redistribution of resources in our country is a core component of our struggle. The struggle is "a worthy set of ideals, but where will the resources come from?" Those who pose this question are themselves usually sitting on the resources. The struggle for redistribution includes: a struggle around government budgeting, ensuring much greater (and more effective) social spending as opposed to, for instance, military spending; and redirecting service provision to the historically oppressed; a reformed tax system; land reform; increasing trade union bargaining power; ensuring that state assets are not stripped and sold to the big corporations. Core state assets need to be democratised and socialised, not privatised. This understanding will not come from the news channels or by reading the corporate-owned newspapers. This has to be taught to the cadre in our ideological schools.

Some leaders erroneously believe that exposing the middle level trade union leaders to all this talk of ideology would take them away from us. The fact is, such an education will cement the bond. And of course who are likely to leave us in case of a discussion on ideology, are not going to be useful to us anyway. The sooner they go, the better. At least all chances of any possible sabotage are being eliminated at a very early stage.

5. Conclusion

The process of building socialism in India has already started. We are into it. We were offered four seats by the then ruling Samajwadi Party and we accepted them. Instead, we should have fought on ninety seats and at least won four. In the process, we would have taken our manifest to a large section of the population. Fortunately by dissociating ourselves from the RJD this time we have saved the morale of our cadre in Bihar. We may not have won a large number of seats, but our strength to fight is intact. This is a very important lesson for us in our future decision-making as far as political adjustments are concerned.

Building socialism through parliamentary democracy is the goal. Winning seats is not. The experience of Nandigram in West Bengal should wake us up from our slumber that once we capture power, everything will happen automatically. Nandigram has proved that eternal vigilance is needed if we really want to build socialism in our country. Being rationalists we have and should have the courage to accept our mistakes. But more important is the need to correct our course whenever such mistakes are being committed. Cohabitation with the capitalist class in a capitalist society is one thing. Being carried away by their market-oriented philosophy is entirely wrong. China has gone this way. West Bengal is on the same track. We must check waywardness of political direction where we have been given the mandate by the working class to decide their future. Even if one farmer or one worker is killed by the police who obey our order, then definitely there is a need to stop and think. As Lenin has said, "Make compromises and the Revolution is lost", we will lose everything if we lose the confidence of the working class after having been bestowed with unmatched faith in the history of parliamentary democracy. Nowhere in the world has a single party of political formation been given such a long unbroken time as in West Bengal in the parliamentary democracy.

The real aim, as said earlier, is to change the foundation of society. Elsewhere, whenever people built socialism, it became more powerful than the other forms of governance. Socialist society had the strength to fight and defeat fascism. It could eliminate internal squabbles. It brought about an unseen equality between men and women. It also gave a sense of dignity to those who were suppressed for centuries. Yet when it came to fighting the enemies within, even such a strong socialist society could not fight them and collapsed.

Eternal vigilance is needed to build a socialist India. Let us begin today, tomorrow may be too late.

6

Socialism in the 20th Century
A Reassessment

Rameshwar Dass and Laxman Singh Shekhawat

The concept of socialism came into existence since the beginning of the modern era in a specific historical context. It was at this time that scholars like Thomas Moore (1478–1535), Saint Simon (1771–1858) and Charles Fourier (1772–1837) saw socialism as a "theory of an ideal society based on equality". They elaborated on the concept in terms of their own social experiences, imaginations and explanations. Some of them, like Robert Owen and Fourier tried to create such a society in their own locality and were impoverished in the process. History called them Utopian Socialists as their efforts and the principles were both based on subjectivism. Despite failure, these thoughts and efforts underlined the need for socialism and created the ground for the future.

It is now an accepted fact that with the rise of Marxism, the scientific theory of socialism also came into being. Marx and Engels had formulated the concept of socialism while developing the theme of dialectical materialism and analysing the principles of motion in human society on the basis of the process of development of the means of production in capitalism. They had visualised that the next phase of development of the developed capitalism would lead towards socialism, but the fact remains that no such revolution has been witnessed in any such country and it certainly needs to be deliberated.

The first proletarian revolution took place in Russia on the basis of principles developed by V.I. Lenin and propounded by Marx and Engels. Lenin had prepared the theoretical grounds of the revolution saying that semi-feudal and semi-industrialised Russia was a weak link in the imperialist stage of capitalism in the world. He had calculated that the "weak link" could be broken easily, and hence led the revolution. It was considered to be the greatest revolution in human history and was taken as the beginning of a new age where capitalism would have met its end and human society would have reached communism after passing through the stage of socialism. At the instance of Lenin, Communist International was formed and the world communist movement received a great impetus and inspiration. In many countries, socialist, communist and democratic parties were formed and later in East Europe, China, Vietnam, Cuba, North Korea and many other countries, socialist and proletarian revolutions took place. It was expected that the wave of communism would spread around the world, but it did not happen. In fact, instead of capitalism, there was the downfall of socialism itself. In the Soviet Union, the social system advanced forward with its achievements and shortcomings, but after seventy years, collapsed like a house of cards. The expectations and hopes of those, who had dreams of socialism and were involved in struggles to achieve it, met with a dead end. The socialist countries in East Europe too faced a similar fate along with Soviet Russia. The countries (Cuba, China, Vietnam, etc.) that could save the system can hardly be called socialist any more.

This is precisely the fate of 20th century socialism. Bourgeois authors saw it as the end of socialism and Marxism. On the other hand, even some Marxist authors have made a superficial analysis of the collapse/ disintegration of the Soviet Union. Some even held just an individual, Gorbachev, responsible for the collapse. In fact not a single step can be taken towards the 21st century (future socialism) without scientifically analysing the 20th century socialism and its principles. There are several reasons for it. Like the first one can be mentioned as the fact that the Communist parties of many countries of the Third World including the Communist Party of India presented the socialism of Soviet Russia as a model for the same. They spent a lot of energy in describing various aspects of it and emphasised that the same system should be replicated elsewhere too. But after the collapse of the Soviet Union, their objective got blurred. The leaders were now not very keen to answer the questions about the structure and content of socialism. Even now the leaders of these Communist parties have no satisfactory explanation. Consequently, the traditional communist movement started getting feeble. The other factor could be identified as the fact that in most of the developing countries, the Communist parties have been working on the lines of the Bolshevik party that later became CPSU and repeated the same mistakes. The scientific analysis of the CPSU and the socialism founded and directed by it could help improve the structure of these parties. In the context of building socialism in the 21st century, it is imperative to go into it.

I

October Revolution and Socialist Programme

The first revolution took place in February (March), 1917

and it was named the democratic revolution under the leadership of the Soviets. It was later led away by parties that supported forces of capitalism, like Mensheviks and the Rightist Democratic Socialist Party and others like them. Under the leadership of the Bolshevik Party, there was another revolution in November in the same year which was called the socialist revolution. In its first decree, private ownership was abolished. It was declared that "All the land will belong to the state, and the plots owned by the royal family, religious institutions, factories, farmers, as well public and private ownership would be confiscated without compensation, would be turned into public property and would serve the interest of the tillers."[1] It was obvious that along with the land of big owners, the small holdings were also nationalised. It was also decreed that there would be control over production and distribution by the state and workers. In the agrarian economy, the collective and state ownership was introduced.

These steps were taken after the revolution towards building socialism and socialising means of production in a country where 75 per cent of the population was illiterate. In non-Russian parts, the situation was even worse. For example, for every 1000 Tajiks, only five were educated, for 48 nationalities, there was no script.[2] In fact, there was acute cultural and economic backwardness. In these parts the development of industrial capitalism was also limited except a few towns of Russia and the influence of Bolsheviks was also confined to these areas only. In February, 1917, there were 24,000 members in this party and out of that, 600 were from Moscow and 2000 from Petrograd or St. Petersburg.[3] In fact, Russia was a semi-feudal and semi- capitalist country and the call of nationalisation had provoked the capitalist, feudal, bureaucratic and militarist elements to issue a call for counter revolution that initiated civil war in the country. The imperialist countries helped the counter revolutionary forces but the Bolshevik Red Army defeated this 'war communism'. However it may be mentioned here that these counter revolutionaries were helped by thousands of small peasants whose land was nationalised. The small peasantry had a significant share in the economy. Their small-scale production had 51 per cent share in the national economy in 1921 and 83 per cent of the toiling population of the country was engaged in handicrafts and small-scale production.[4]

It can be said that one of the main reasons for the expansion of the counter revolutionary forces was the taking away of the means of production from the small producers that forced them into the ranks of the reactionaries. The peasants lost interest in agriculture. The rate of production started coming down heavily. Even after winning over the civil war, the revolution faced a constant threat from small producers, especially the small peasantry and petty bourgeoisie.

It is clear that in a country where the productive forces were far less developed than in the existing capitalist countries, socialism could be brought only as an alternative and not as a step ahead, and that too was done far too soon. Lenin had anticipated the consequences and had started making reforms since as early as in 1918. Immediately after gaining control over the civil war, he announced "New Economic Policy", known as NEP in 1921[5] which has its own significance in the socialist history of Russia. In the course of civil war itself in 1918, he wrote his famous book, *Leftwing Communism, an Infantile Disorder*. The chapter called "The Present Economic System in Russia" became the background for NEP. Lenin had presented in this chapter a new formulation of state capitalism before constructing socialism.[6] It was taken as a better way of transition towards socialism for the backward countries like Russia taking in various elements from their socio-economic structures and developing a specific economy. Lenin wrote, "...The state capitalism is decidedly more advanced compared to our present economic progress."[7] Lenin had further written in the context of how the small producers and petty bourgeoisie had turned against socialism after the declaration of the "socialist programme" at the time of the civil war, "Capitalism is not fighting against socialism, instead the petty bourgeoisie and private capitalism together are fighting against state capitalism and socialism. The petty bourgeoisie always stands against any government control or restrain irrespective of its being either state capitalism or state socialism."[8]

Lenin defined, the new economic policy in his book *Tax in Kind,* which is a historical document. Lenin had tried to correct the preliminary mistakes in it committed after the revolution. He had understood that hurrying things would not help. The Bolsheviks would be isolated in society if they tried to force matters. He emphasised that a material, social and cultural base must be prepared for socialism He also stressed further development of the means of production as well as their productivity.[9] He wrote, "Without capitalist technology, based on the advanced scientific discoveries, socialism is not possible." He also talked about taking tax in kind and the sale of surplus production in the market. In contrast to the declarations made in the early days of revolution, he even supported, to an extent, the resurrection of the petty bourgeois and capitalist classes based on free trade. He wrote," We should not try to put an end to the progress of capitalism, instead we should try to turn it towards state capitalism. It is possible from the economic point of view because state capitalism is always present wherever there is any existence of free trade and elements of capitalism."[10] Lenin also stressed learning of management skills and other economic expertise. He had also kept an eye over the rise of bureaucracy in the Soviet regime. About how to conduct economic activities, he wrote, "We should not be afraid to accept the fact that we still have to learn a lot from capitalists, and in fact we should try to learn."[11]

The small industrialists and traders were allowed to continue with their own business. He also emphasised foreign capital investment in Russia. Such companies were given facilities for trade and were permitted to open their own factories. At the 11th Congress of the Bolshevik Party, Lenin informed the members about the decision to have large-scale cooperation with foreign companies. He mentioned the foundation of nine mixed companies and 17 big foreign companies.[12] He stressed learning of economic management and joining together with the world market system. Clearly he had realised the mistakes committed during the process of revolution and the consequent enthusiasm. He was revising the wrongs fast, and soon positive results were visible. Russia started moving ahead on the path of mixed capitalist economic system. A system was emerging with private and state capitalism, which had a tendency to move towards socialism after crossing over the stage of state capitalism. If this policy continued, the future of Russia would have been different. But this did not happen as Stalin's understanding had brought into existence a totally opposite system.

The End of NEP, and Stalin's Economic System

After Lenin got ill in 1922, Stalin became the first general secretary of the party, a post which till then did not exist, even in the underground days. In his leadership, NEP started getting feeble. By 1928, it was totally transformed. The democratic development of the economic system was changed according to personal whims and desires. The construction of socialism was speeded up following cruel suppression and extreme policies. The land was grabbed from the small peasants calling them "kulaks." In some places, even chicken and cattle were taken away to collective farms. In as short span of two years; land at all levels and factories were collectivised and nationalised. Farming was socialised and heavily industrialised violating all the standards of industrial economy.[13]

It was attributed a theoretical format calling it a historical need to fight imperialism.[14] Under the formulation, a process of transition was unleashed with inhuman cruelties and a section justifies these steps even today. It may be mentioned that in the period between 1928–34, tens of lakhs of farmers starved to death.[15] Agricultural production went down. The peasants were forced inhumanly to slog in the construction of buildings, railways, roads and electricity generation. Such labour was called "socialist labour" or "spontaneous collective labour." In fact it was an unpaid labour that was forced in conditions of starvation and semi-starvation. Within a decade of such economic and cultural transition, it was claimed that Russia had crossed the stage of socialism, and the country was moving towards communism.[16]

We should consider as to what extent it was socialism. Several issues came up in this context. First of all, was this method of construction of socialism in Soviet Russia justifiable? The answer is negative in our view. Millions of people faced extreme cruelties but it was not all. The seeds of the collapse of the Soviet system could be traced in these extremities. The policies of 'great leap' adopted by Stalin (later adopted by Mao) was in total opposition to the policy adopted by Lenin and to the post-revolution objective situation. Lenin had suggested painstaking development of work-culture and of the material conditions of science and technology. Any haste in this regard only opened the way to bureaucracy and unrestricted domination. Lenin was aware of the growing deterioration in the Soviet Union. Subjective methods of building socialism could only lead to bureaucracy. The basic administrative machinery was still Tsarist in nature (Lenin had already pointed this out after the revolution). Improvement in it was not so easy.[17] Of particular importance, in this context, was the fact that the peasants and workers, supposed to bring revolution, were backward. Therefore, they were not in a position to create better administration. They lacked knowledge, training and education. Therefore, as opposed to Stalin, Lenin emphasised development of proper culture, with great patience and sobriety. He warned against haste: "It is necessary to remember that this lack of knowledge cannot be covered up with haste and maddening super enthusiasm,"[19]

In fact, this very fact has proved to be the most destruction factor in the 20th century.

Therefore, Lenin, on the one hand, emphasised the need for improving state administration. To this end, he suggested formation of workers'-peasants' inspection. On the other hand, he suggested creating advanced and conscious workers, who would follow the dictum of Lenin: 'learn again and again and again'. He warned that 'science' should not become a fashionable word to be uttered again and again. (Let us remind ourselves that we do precisely this!). A scientific attitude should become an inalienable part of ourselves.[20]

Haste was, in Lenin's view, the greatest danger. 'Let us not be miserly on time, and let us take necessary time to do things', he stated.21 Culture was to be taken to great heights. Objective conditions should be taken into account. 'Examine properly and move ahead carefully', he said. "Measure the cloth seven times at least before you cut it out."[22] But Stalin did not pay heed: he began cutting the cloth without measuring it at all! He wanted communism to be built overnight! Consequently, the workers and peasants lost power, which was concentrated first in the hands of the party, then the central committee and ultimately in the hands of Stalin. A centralised bureaucracy and dictatorship was created in the name of the working class and its party. Democracy was destroyed completely within the party. Not only the dissent but the dissenters themselves were destroyed and physically eliminated. Top leaders like Zinoviev, Kamenev, Bukharin, Raikov, Tomsky, Trotsky,, etc. simply disappeared, eliminated physically.[23]

A highly rigid centralised and repressive bureaucracy was created in the country. The country was at the mercy of a handful of people, headed by Stalin. These decisions were taken in the name of "Construction of Socialism or Communism" and implemented by a centralised bureaucracy.[24]

After the death of Stalin in 1953, the central committee of the CPSU passed a proposal on Overcoming the Cult of the Individual and its Consequences. In a suppressed spirit and balanced way, the individual worship in the party was criticised and Stalin was held responsible for it. The atrocities committed by Beria and his gang were also attacked.[25] But the bureaucracy developed in the regime of Stalin and known as the Stalinist system had taken very deep roots. It was not possible to uproot it easily.

Here the question arises how a party of the proletariat lost its hold and surrendered to the dictatorship of Stalin? There is no doubt that the Bolshevik Party was revolutionary. The principles on which the party was organised to fight feudal militarism were not wrong. No liberal party could have succeeded at that time. There was certainly a need for cadre-based organisation. But the possibility of the misuse of power was ingrained in this organisation only and Rosa

Luxemburg had expressed her fear about it long ago.[26] After Stalin became general secretary, Lenin had anticipated the dangers. He witnessed in his last days the end of flexibility and democracy in the party that had remained intact even in the difficult days of the underground period. In the principles "democratic centralism", democracy was disappearing and was being replaced by centralism. He wrote several letters to the party centre in this context, out of which several were brought to light only after his death. He had written, "Stalin is rude and for the post of general secretary, it is intolerable."[27] For this very reason, he had suggested Stalin's removal from the post. He had written on December 24, 1922, "Com. Stalin has acquired endless powers in his hands after becoming general secretary and I am not sure if he would be able to use it with caution."

In his letter "In the name of the Congress,"[28] he wrote, "I want to suggest strongly that there should be several organisational changes made in this Congress in our political structure of the party."[29] Lenin was in no way narrow about the party organisation. He was stressing the need of changes to be made in the political structure of the party according to the changing situation. Very few Communist parties in many countries formed on the basis of Bolshevik principles have paid any heed to this fact. Their organisational structure has remained unchanged till now. Lenin had said in this context, "I place the need on top of everything else, of increasing the number of central committee members upto several dozens, it would go even to a hundred."[30] About increasing the number, he wrote, "The party needs to be careful about the increasing importance of the factions among the small factions inside the central committee and it is imperative to put a stop to it for the personnel of party work seriously."[31] Thus Lenin wanted to restrain the struggle for power by increasing the membership of the central committee. He wanted to get these members, which could be fifty to hundred in number, from among those who came from the working class and peasantry and were working directly among the masses at a lower level after the Soviet revolution. Lenin had written, "Those who are active in the ranks, lower than the levels created in the last five years inside the units of Soviet units, and are closer to ordinary workers and peasants but do not get identified with the groups of exploiters either directly or indirectly."[32] He was never in favour for taking those who were active for long inside the Soviet organisations. Because in his opinion, "They had become victims of several traditions, were biased against many things and it was imperative to fight against them."[33] He strongly believed that "several dozens of workers could join our central committee and after examining our field and methods of activities, could easily reform and reconstruct it and they could be much better at it than many things."[34]

Therefore the party and Soviet regime had to make it democratic in the real sense to become a proletariat power. Lenin had tried hard and offered suggestions that could never be implemented and was always interrupted by Stalin's hunger for power. He became a real tyrant with his conspiracies and oppressive methods. It proved to be one of the main factors that led to the collapse of the Soviet regime in Russia. The other question that emerges here is whether Stalin or the Soviet regime after him could develop the productive forces sufficiently. There is no doubt about the landmark achievements of Soviet power in building basic and large industries, railways, electricity and its expansion and the armaments, though people had to pay heavily for all these measures. But it was a subjective and one-sided development of the productive forces. The development was exclusively based on the needs of the Soviet regime.

The needs of the common man were never considered. It is obvious in the sphere of production of consumer goods. The scientific-technological revolution and the development of information technology in the capitalist countries went unheeded in the then Soviet Union and contributed to the collapse of the system, which was the socialism of the 20th century. The productive forces lagged behind compared to those in capitalist countries in reaching the qualitative stages of development and led to the backwardness of the Soviet system.

There was a double impact of both STR and IT. It brought to light the weaknesses of the Soviet system as well as the realities of much higher standards of common life in the capitalist countries compared to the people of Russia. The Russian people started thirsting for openness. All these factors had their own significance in the process of collapse of the socialist system of Russia.

Now the question arises why the Socialist system in Russia and other countries failed to develop the productive forces as much as in capitalist countries? Why did it then lag behind? Usually the explanation is given that in the process of struggle against imperialism and aid extended to the newly independent countries in the world that came out of imperialist oppression, the system had been too involved to care for these needs. But the reasoning is not adequate; serious deliberation is needed on these points, especially on the lack of the market system. The classical Marxist concepts have mentioned the routing of market. It was the follow up of the understanding that after socialisation of means of production, commodity production would end, which meant that society would produce according to the needs.[35] But in the practical experience of two yeas after the October Revolution, there were several changes in the concept of market for Lenin. He had started accepting the importance of market and private enterprises in the backward and small-scale producing countries like Russia.[36] But in the days of Stalin, they were totally abolished. The same things happened in China and other socialist countries.

The market system is not meant for reducing the gap between the consumer and the producer alone,[37] but it also serves as an indicator of the needs and decrees of the consumers. In the absence of this system, natural development of productive forces is stalled. The party units and especially the central committee could never decide to remove these shortcomings, since their influence was more of a subjective nature with negative impressions. US Communist Party leader Sam Webb has come to the conclusion that even if the revolution takes place in the advanced countries, the need for the market system will exist. Says Webb, "Even if we are dealing with more advanced countries—take our country, for example—if this were the day after, the week after, the year after, the decade after the socialist revolution, we would employ market mechanisms in the construction of the socialist system."[38] There is also lack of democracy. The content of socialism should always have been democracy. It should always be so. Democracy was lacking in the Soviet system and in other Soviet-type countries. In the name of proletarian dictatorship, real power was concentrated in the hands of the party, central committee and ultimately the general secretary. A rigid bureaucracy managed the administration. The real power was not in the hands of the working class or working people. They did not have the right to political criticism, nor did the system have any critical checks and balances. Even if we leave out the period of War Communism or the Second World War and other periods of emergencies, the people did not have rights of democratic nature in the normal, peaceful times. The criticism of the leaders and of the bureaucracy was not tolerated. There was no forum and freedom for discussion and criticism of the political questions and of the leaders. The socialist electoral system did not represent people's opinions and wishes in real terms. The people's representatives did not represent the public will, there was no place for the opposition. Democracy was virtually absent within the party.

The direct multi-party electoral system alone can be the real representative of the people's will. In reality, a system was required to uncover the deficiencies of the system and the mistakes, so that the communists could improve themselves and prove better among the people again and again. Such a system was needed to measure the extent of people's support for the communists. The elections held in the recent years in the ex-USSR and the countries of Eastern Europe are a pointer to this. In Russia, the Communist Party base received only about 11% of votes, and in the countries of Eastern Europe 20 to 25% of votes.

There were possibilities for the multi-party system in Russia after the February Revolution (1917). This clearly represented a transition from feudalism to capitalism. Power passed into the hands of the Bolsheviks. The counter-revolution used violence to overthrow this power. In such a situation, the Constituent Assembly was dissolved on January 7, 1918, because it refused to recognise the Soviet power. Since then, one-party rule was in existence in the Soviet Union till 1991. After the extraordinary war situations were over, multi-party system or more democratic structure should have been created. One should note that though the countries calling themselves socialist, e.g. China, Vietnam,, etc. are carrying out large-scale economic reforms, but they refuse to carry out political reforms. Therefore, the people had to pay a heavy price for the so-called socialist construction earlier, as also today for these reforms. Facts are coming to the fore in this regard despite internal censorship.[39]

Thus, the absence of market mechanism and of democracy, have been two serious problems for socialism in the 20th century.

II

We have so far evaluated the practical side of the 20^{lh} century socialism. Now, we return to the basic question: 'Why has socialism not emerged as a higher and better level of social development' compared to capitalism in any of the advanced capitalist country/countries of the West, so far? That is how Marx and Engels visualised the question. Lenin also was of the opinion that capitalism had reached its highest stage, i.e. imperialism which was the eve of socialism.[40]

In the *Communist Manifesto* and several subsequent writings (e.g. *Capital, Civil War in France, Socialism: Utopian and Scientific,* etc.), Marx and Engels repeatedly reach the conclusion that the basic crisis of capitalism can only be solved by socialism. They analysed deeply the various aspects of capitalism. They found that the growing collectivity of labour was coming into increasing conflict with the private ownership of the means of production, and that this could not go on for ever. This crisis of labour and of capital was a hurdle in the path of development of the productive forces. The contradiction could be resolved in only one way—by establishing social ownership of the means of production by the socialised labour. This was looked upon as the socialist or communist system. To reach there, the proletariat had to organise itself as a political force. That is why, Marx-Engels emphasised the political organisation of the proletariat. They themselves took active part in the political organisations of the working class. They also took personal part in organising the proletariat. During their lifetime, the only proletarian revolution was the Paris Commune (1871). Though they considered that there were potentials of proletarian revolution in Germany, France, etc., in the 19th century, but it did not really take place.

The crisis and contradiction of labour and capital, as seen by Marx, Engels and Lenin, were not a figment of the imagination, capitalism also went through general crises on several occasions, but it was always successful in coming out of them. Capitalism has always overcome its crises with the help of new and higher technologies. World 'capitalism was able to overcome the crises of the world wars and fascism, and reach new levels of development.

After the Second World War, particularly that last 30–40 years, a scientific and technological revolution (STR) has taken place. The basic contradiction has been solved in a way different from the proletarian revolution. Science and technology have themselves become a major production force.[41] STR is separating the labour process from the productive process. Now, production and distribution are increasingly taking recourse to the microprocessors and computers. Information processing works somewhat like the human brain, but much faster. This distinguishes it from the industrial automatic machines, which take their own decisions regarding processes of coordination, direction, managing, etc. This is a qualitative change in the development of the productive forces.[42] It has left behind the industrial stage of social development. The industrial society can be seen only in some areas. Even then, some dogmatist communists and Maoists still harbour Utopian dreams of a proletarian revolution.

Marx did pay attention to the separation of labour process from the production process. None other than him could go into the depths of the capitalist system of production. This is accepted by even the academics of the advanced western capitalist countries. It is to be noted that Marx in his *Grundrisse*[43] gives indications of the disappearance of the labour process due to automation. During those times, there was no sign of electronics. He wrote: "After entering the capitalist mode of production, the means of labour undergo a series of changes, that lead ultimately to the emergence of the automatic machine system. This automatic system is self-acting. The automation is the result of several mechanical and intellectual processes, whereby the worker is pushed outside the production process just as an observer."

Not only this, Marx notes as to how labour is reduced to only certain moments in the production process. He writes, "Production process is no more labour process because now it no more is the labour-creating process. Labour now is only a conscious element, spread over various points of production." This was, in fact, a scientific social analysis of the mechanical age. We can only visualise that had Marx lived today in the electronic age, how precise he would have been, and what he would have said in the context of socialism, and what type of socialism. Would he have talked of 'proletarian dictatorship'? We must think over it.

III

As we have stated earlier, we cannot properly develop the concepts of 21st century socialism without taking proper lessons from the 20th century socialism. Lessons of the past are useful for the future.

We may demarcate certain points for the discussion:

1. The earliest socialist revolution took place in the backward, semi-feudal and semi-capitalist countries. Socialism was sought to be developed not as a higher

stage of social development after capitalism, but as an 'alternative' to capitalism.

2. This method of socialist construction was not an objective, natural one. It was more a subjective attempt.
3. Consequently, the production forces developed one-sidedly. A backward country like the Soviet Union did develop into a 'super power' of the world, but its downfall was also inherent in this very subjective process.
4. Absence of democracy in the party and the society, as also lack of market did not help develop productive forces as per the wishes of the people. Therefore, despite being a superpower, the USSR (i.e. Socialism) kept falling behind capitalism. Socialism could not race ahead of capitalism in competition. As a consequence, it was socialism that collapsed, not capitalism.
5. Since socialism of the 20th century fell behind in the field of STR, it could not enter the qualitatively higher stage (post-industrial society) of social development. So, socialism fell one whole era behind. Therefore, its fall was inevitable.
6. The rest of the socialist countries (China, Vietnam,, etc.) are going through a transition period to the post-industrial society. But the absence of democracy is making this transition extremely painful. Besides, their development too is not natural.
7. Now, there is no possibility of a proletarian revolution in any country because its theoretical basis—the crisis of labour and capital—has disappeared. This crisis has been resolved by the STR, due to which the labour forces have separated from the production process.

Consequently, the revolutionary forces of the industrial age, the proletariat is no more in existence.

8. In the post-industrial age, the main problem is not that of the socialisation or nationalisation of the means of production. Now, the main centre of attention should be distribution and the environmental question. Democratic and civil society's struggle today has become an historical necessity. The class struggle is no more the main form of struggle. Mass people's struggle is now the main form. According to the CP USA, "Socialism is not just a project of the left; it has to be a mass project of millions and of diverse social forces."[44] Pressures through democratic processes can be increased. Civil society can now play a more active role. STR is reaching new heights. Their combination renders the revolution not as some instant moment but a prolonged process. This objective process is moving towards communism. The objective hurdles in its path have to be removed—imperialism, fascism, bureaucracy, corruption, etc. This is the function that the subjective forces can discharge.
9. In the 1880s, Marx had talked of 'buying off' the capitalist class. This is quite applicable in today's conditions of moving towards communism. Lenin had interpreted this formulation in the conditions when bureaucracy and military groups would be very weak; therefore, socialism could be achieved peacefully.[45]

Conclusion

Therefore, we conclude that today, we need a powerful mass progressive, people's movement. We must free ourselves of all the limitations of the industrial age (including left sectarianism). We should assimilate the positive aspects of that age. This should include not only economic and social but cultural respects too. The process should have close interaction with means of information and media. We should follow the dictum of 'Learn, Unlearn and Relearn'. Democratic thought process and programme are absolutely essential and the first priority.

Otherwise, extremist forces like the fascist, terrorist, left adventurism, i.e. Naxalism, etc. will emerge, and are already emerging, as hurdles to social development.

References

1. Lenin, "Report on the Land Question" (October 26, 1917), *CW* 26, pp. 257–60.
2. A. Ugrayumov, *Building of Socialism in the Soviet Union: Lenin's Plan (1917–25)*, Delhi, 1977, pp. 28–29.
3. Anil Rajimwale, *Scientific and Technological Revolution and the Post-Industrial Society*, Delhi University, 1997, p. 13 (in Hindi).
4. Ugrayumov, p. 50.
5. Lenin, *CW* 3, Pt 2, 1967, pp. 202–240.
6. Lenin had identified five socio-economic formations in the Russian society after revolution: Natural patriarchal agrarian, small-scale commodity production (involving most of the peasants), private capitalism, state capitalism, and socialist. Ibid. (Hindi, free translation).
7. At present, Russia is dominated by petty capitalism. This leads to both state capitalism and socialism. There is the common intermediate station: "The social management and regulation of production and distribution", *Lenin, CW* 3, Pt 2, p. 207 (Hindi, free translation).
8. Ibid., p. 203.
9. Ibid., p. 206.
10. Ibid.
11. Ibid.
12. Lenin, *On Peaceful Coexistence*, Moscow 1975, p. 58.
13. See, Charles Bettelheim, *Class Struggles in the USSR*, in 4 vols. T.R. Publications, 1994.
14. "Encirclement of the Soviet Union, the civil war, the preparation for the Second World War by the fascist forces, did not allow the Soviet Union a peaceful period necessary for a protracted transition

towards the consolidation of socialist productive forces. Sitaram Yechury, "21st Century and Socialist China", at the International Symposium on World Socialism in the 21st Century, Beijing, 2002.

15. Bettelheim, op. cit.
16. Constitution of the USSR, 1936.
17. Lenin, Better Fewer But Better.
18. Ibid.
19. Ibid.
20. Ibid.
21. Ibid.
22. Ibid.
23. Anil Rajimwale, op. cit.
24. Ibid.
25. *On Overcoming the Cult of the Individual and its Consequences,* Roxy Press, New Delhi.
26. Rosa Luxemburg, *The Russian Revolution: Leninism or Marxism?,* The University of Michigan Press, 1972.
27. V.I. Lenin, Letters to the Congress, *CW* 10 (Hindi).
28. Ibid.
29. Ibid.
30. Ibid.
31. Ibid.
32. Ibid.
33. Ibid.
34. Ibid.
35. V.I. Lenin, Marx, Critique of Gotha Programme, *SW* 3. *Engels, Socialism: Utopian and Scientific, CW* 15, p. 138.
36. Lenin, *SW* 3, Pt 2, pp. 202–240 (Hindi).
37. Alvin Toffler, *Third Wave.*
38. Sam Webb, Democracy Matters: An Interview with Sam Webb, *Political Affairs Magazine,* January 2004.
39. From the speech of the Chinese delegate at the AIYF Conference, Sirsa, Haryana, 2007.
40. Lenin, *Imperialism: The Highest Stage of Capitalism.*
41. Rajimwale, op cit.
42. Ibid.
43. Marx, *Grundrisse.*
44. Sam Webb, op. cit.
45. Lenin, On the Present Situation in Russia, *SW* 3.

7

Socialism in the 21st Century

C.R. Bakshi

The lessons of building socialism in the 20th century in the erstwhile Soviet Union has made the communists throughout the world wiser in searching for their own path of building socialism in their respective countries in the 21st century, according to the level of economic and social development of their respective economies and the class alignment of forces in the multiple superstructure obtaining in each country.

The course of development of socialism will vary from country to country, though the direction will be common to reach the goal of scientific socialism where a system will be created by the state, which, according to Marx, "will unleash the full development of all human potential". While in the economic field, it will create enough wealth to be distributed equitably by the state, politically, as Chavez has said: "One of the determining factors of the 21st century will be participatory democracy, a popular power in which everything has to be centred in the people, where the party must be subordinated to the people, not the other way round." Clarifying this point, the Bolivarian vice-president Alvaro Garcia Lineria said recently: "The idea of state implies the concentration of decision-making. The state has a monopoly in that area. But the term social movement signifies diffusion of decision-making, socialisation of the process. Perhaps it is these tensions between socialisation and concentration, between democratisation of decision-making and monopoly, through which revolutions of the 21^{s1} century will have to proceed."

The Communist Party of India has dropped the old concept of proletarian dictatorship long ago and the party constitution provides that it will allow opposition in parliament in a multi-party system of governance.

The 21st century will be a period of many human endeavours of building socialism according to the specific characteristics of different countries in the world. Actually, for the under developed and developing economies, even after the replacement of bourgeois rule, the capitalist mode of production and distribution through the market will remain in operation for a long time as a means of increase and development of productive forces. This has the theoretical backing of none else other than Lenin, who during the period of the New Economic Policy (NEP), after the October Revolution, said: "It means that to a certain extent, we are recreating capitalism. We are doing this quite openly. It is state capitalism. But state capitalism in a state where power belongs to capital and state capitalism in a society where power belongs to the proletariat are two different concepts. In a capitalist state, state capitalism means that it is recognised by the state and controlled by it for the benefit of the bourgeoisie and to the detriment of the proletariat. In the proletarian state, the same thing is done for the benefit of the working class for the purpose of withstanding the as yet strong bourgeoisie and of fighting it. It goes without saying that we must give concessions to the foreign bourgeoisie, to foreign capital. Without the slightest denationalisation, we shall lease mines, forests and oil fields to foreign capitals and receive in exchange manufactured goods, machinery etc., and thus restore our own industry." (Lenin *Collected Works,* Vol. 32, p. 491) This was said by Lenin about 81 years ago, when the world and its economy, politics and the correlation of social forces were different, when STR and ICR did not appear in the sense of the present dimension.

Now when China and Vietnam take the course of building socialism by accepting Lenin's NEP, many new contradictions and constraints have appeared within the capitalist system. STR and ICR coupled with globalisation of the economies and markets have thrown up new problems and new questions which are to be addressed. The NEP suggested by Lenin was not put into practice. So, there is no past experience of that time of its application in building socialism. But as Lenin said: "We must face this issue squarely—who will come out on top? Either the capitalists succeed in organising first—in which case they will drive out the communists and that will be the end of it. Or, the proletarian state power, with the support of the peasantry, will prove capable of keeping a proper rein on these gentlemen, the capitalists, so as to direct capitalism along state channels and to create a capitalism that will be subordinate to the state and serve the state. (Lenin *Collected Works,* Vol. 33, p. 66)

The Chinese leader Deng Xiaoping, in support of the Chinese experiment of Socialist Market Economy, said that "the crux of the matter is not whether the road is capitalist or socialist. The chief criterion of making that judgment should be whether it helps to promote the growth of productive forces in a socialist society": He himself raised the question: "Is it possible that a new bourgeoisie will emerge?" In reply, he himself said, "a handful of bourgeois elements may appear, but they will not form a class. Our reform requires that we keep public ownership predominant and guard against polarisation." (*Selected Works of Deng*, Vol. 3, pp. 142–143)

Clearly, we can see, this line followed by the CPC is in conformity with Lenin's NEP and in particular with Marxism-Leninism in general. Lenin had developed his policy of acceptance of the market economy for using this in a backward economy, where productive forces were to be developed speedily through competition in the market and also to learn from the developed Western capitalist economy how to build industry and manage it efficiently. He wanted to direct his NEP to learn from the capitalist class and also to compete with them.

The forces of socialism in the countries like India will have to learn from lessons of Chinese and Vietnam experiments with socialist market economy to build socialism in the 21st century with their own characteristics. For that matter, Vietnam with far less developed productive forces had to learn from the mistakes of both the Soviet and Chinese model. The Communist Party of Vietnam is now engaged in the job of rectifying their past mistakes by following the course of building socialism through their own socialist market economy named Doi Moi, meaning 'innovation'. Since 1986, after 10 years of beginning the Chinese experiment on market economy. By the end of nearly 20 years of Doi Moi, Vietnam has achieved great successes in increasing their productive forces to a large extent. The Indian Communists are fortunate that they will be benefited from the experiences of China and Vietnam in building socialism in the 21st century with Indian characteristics.

As for the developed countries, many people seem to be pessimistic. But they forget that the law of contradiction in exploitation is inherent and the globalisation, neo-liberalism, imperialism, war economy, growth of finance capital, unemployment, increasing gap between rich and poor, global terrorism—all these are the symptoms of capitalist crises. Even with the STR and ICR as new tools in hand and capitalism cannot sustain for long. These are helping socialisation of labour power extensively. New social forces are being gathered in larger numbers around the world as the left, socialists and communists fight back the capitalist offensive including that in USA. Without going into the details, one can predict safely that in the rapid growth of productive forces and economic development in developing economies in socialist China, Vietnam and also in Latin America, though in many cases, this growth is to a large extent due to the capitalist world coupled with STR and ICR, but the contradiction between the productive forces and production relations and the distribution of wealth will be dampened. This we have learnt from the fundamentals of Marxism-Leninism. As the competition between the socialist market economy and the classical capitalist economy will grow, the crisis of the capitalist system will deepen further and revolutionary upsurge in the West will engulf the capitalist supremacy and for socialist revolution. In what form it will come, is a matter of the future.

Though it cannot be predicted now as to what will be the real stage of socialist development in the coming 92 years of the 21st century, it is certain that more and more socialist countries will emerge in this century; who will decisively compete with capitalist countries—that will yet remain in the scene and alternatively, the doom of capitalism is inevitable.

Let us hope that socialism in a larger part of the world will attain its supremacy over capitalism by the end of the 21st century and humanity will march forward towards communism with the advent of the 22nd century, a sketch of which was drawn by Mahapandit Rahul Sankrutyayan in his famous book *Viswai Shanthi,* written in Hindi.

8

Gender Question in Marxist Paradigm

Krishna Jha

It is an attempt to look into the past from present to analyse the future, not only in terms of the periodicity but also in taking up contemporary discourse and its relationship with the woman question.

Woman was the first slave even before slaves existed. She faced "the historical defeat" when man started making his own tools and used them for not only satisfying hunger but also for prosperity. The days of food gathering and agriculture by hand were gone and came the end of matriarchy. She was dethroned. She lagged behind as the instruments of labour kept getting heavier and the process itself got too complicated. Her marginalisation was explained as "natural inferiority" and her existence was recognised as an afterthought, created from a "spare rib".

The class position of financially dependent women is never clear. As the making of means of production advanced, women were thrown into the background—they lost their domination as matriarchy ended and monogamy as well as private property was initiated. They got the status of a private servant as the seeds of first antagonism were noticed in the socio-economic formation. Thus, physical incapacity deterred women from joining the making and progress of means of production and their use. In course of time, they were increasingly confined in the four walls of their homes. The sphere of production was totally dominated by men. It was the historical defeat of the female sex, as Engels had put it.

He dominated over the production process; she was thrown into the background. Explanations, given to justify the unequal division in feudalism, capitalism varied saying that women's brains were smaller than men's, their physical formation was of a different shape, they were governed by their emotions, less rational than men.

The explanations, though popular, were not enough to explain everything. For example, the difference between men and women's wages was justified saying men did work which was more physically demanding. But even among men, when it came to allocating wages and salaries, physical strength was devalued in favour of dexterity and skill or intellectual activity. She was taken either as a goddess and worshipped or as a slave and belittled. She was never accepted as an equal. She was always given the role, which linked her with the family. Man, his dependent wife and dependent children—has always existed and said to be the natural and best way of organising society. Charles Fourier was right when he said, "The degree of emancipation of women is the natural measure of general emancipation."

Marx took it further when he said that the degree of emancipation of women reflected the progress of human over animal and culture over nature. It was taken as an index of general social advance. But the quest for the emancipation of women, with its universal importance, lost its specific content and was given a subsidiary status in course of time.

The explanation for this could be traced in the lack of focus on the crucial issue. It is not without reason, therefore, that August Babel, in his "Women in the Past, Present and Future", admitted that even in the socialist classics this debate is not taken up as one of the basic issues, but only in terms of generalised philosophical formulations, or as part of specific historical analysis of family, within the context of economy as well as evolution of property.

The mainstream belief led one to assume that the division of labour between men and women was natural, slaves to their biology, especially women facing restraints at every level, thinking of themselves as only childbearers, while men naturally played the role of providers and protectors. Any attempt to depart from the stand by women was to have its own consequences.

In the class society, to maintain the control over the society, the beginning was made from the smallest unit, the unit of a family, where the members were to respect the authority. The obedience to authority starts from the household and reaches the wider limits of the society, the state, and the ruling forces. The pattern was followed by even Soviet Russia under the leadership of Joseph Stalin, who made a retreat from the communal provision of services and care which otherwise women had to do in their households. The trend had its roots in the need of the bureaucracy to maintain a stable hierarchy of relations and thereby impose restraints on the 'subservient' forces.

Whereas the Bolshevik Revolution set women free, Stalinism led to a drastic reversal of policy on women and the family. Many of the gains made by the revolution were abolished. Abortions were made illegal and divorce was made increasingly difficult till it became an expensive court procedure. Prostitutes were arrested, whereas the early Bolshevik policy had been to arrest only the brothel owners and expose the men who bought prostitutes and to provide voluntary job training for the prostitutes. The hours of day-care centres were cut down to coincide with the hours of the working day. Female children were taught special subjects in the schools to prepare them for their role as mothers and housewives.

The ideal family in a class-divided society is a unit based on the economic dependence of "non-productive" members of the household on an individual wage earner, traditionally the man, who has been identified as the head of the household. Lower wages for women was justified because work was taken as secondary to bringing up a family. A woman would spend most of her adult life dependent financially on a male breadwinner; therefore, she could be paid merely "pin money", and any attempt to deviate from this role by women remaining single, for example, or by living as single parent family would lead to socially disastrous consequences.

The obvious implication of this, very useful to capitalism, is that the full financial burden is borne by the family without recourse to the state. The family, of course, does not have the material or psychological resources to carry such burdens. At various points in history this led to starvation, malnourishment and disease.

However, this fragile system of sustenance for wives is gradually disappearing as more women are going out to work and share the family expenses. There are also situations, when families have no choices left except either perishing or leaving. The man leaves without qualms, while the woman continues to shoulder the burden of the entire household, in the same harrowing circumstances. And yet, the role of patriarchy or the institutionalised dominance of men in society remains valid.

Engels wrote his book, *The Origins of the Family, Private Property and the State,* at a time when official ideology pointed to a natural division of labour between women as the carers, slaves to their biology, restricted in what they do and even the way they think by their role as childrearers; and men, who 'naturally' participated in public life, went out to work as the providers and protectors of their dependents. Any attempt to depart from this by women would have terrible repercussions. But it was a moment of transition. Capitalism needed women as cheap and skilled workforce to toil on the new machines. Women were needed to establish the factory system, in the developing textile and service industries. Women were drawn out from their allocated sphere to slog in the factory.

The industrial revolution leading to the birth of capitalist wage-labour enabled women to be equal to men in social production, and also liberated them from domestic labour. But to bring the whole female sex back into public industry meant the end of private property and for this the characteristic of the monogamous family as the economic unit of society was also to be abolished. It was not acceptable. Hence the various checks and restraints.

In the larger context, women's emancipation remained relative and was seen only as a result of consequent social development. Her experience was never taken as raw material but only through various interpretations. As early as in the 19th century, Marx had pointed out that there would always be the tendency in capitalism to make super profits from the exploitation of women and children. In the first volume of *Capital,* Marx wrote: "The labour of women and children was, therefore, the first thing sought for by capitalists who used machinery. That mighty substitute for labour and labourers was forthwith changed into a means for increasing the number of wage-labourers by enrolling, under the direct sway of capital, every member of the workman's family, without distinction of age or sex. Compulsory work for the capitalist usurped the place, not only of the children's play, but also of free labour at home within moderate limits for the support of the family." (Karl Marx, *Capital,* Vol. 1. pp. 394–5.)

With the electronic revolution, the mode of production has undergone a further transition, and made it easier for women to play a significant role in the process. With the widening venues for employment, there is growing requirement for women who are subjected to the worst kind of exploitation, working for low wages in abysmal conditions with few or no rights. In America alone, some 40 million women have joined the workforce over the past 50 years; in Europe another 30 million. In 1950, only about a third of all American women of working age had a paid job; last year the proportion was nearly three-quarters.

The very fact that women are able to come out and get involved in highly skilled jobs is, in itself, a progressive development. It is the prior condition to the liberation of women from the four walls called home, and a step towards their blossoming free as human beings and members of society. However there is the other side as well. The system has placed women merely as a convenient source of cheap labour, sometimes forming a "pool" from which labour can be drawn whenever there is a shortage of labour in specific areas of production, and discarded again when the need disappears.

Both the world wars have brought to light the dreaded fact that women were engaged in the factories to replace men who had been called up into the army and then sent back to the home when the war ended. Women were again encouraged to enter the workplaces during the upswing of the 1950s and 1960s, but were given the status of the immigrant workers—as a reservoir of cheap labour. In the more recent period, there have been laizedws to guarantee equality, but there is no end to the exploitation of women workers who remain the most oppressed section of the proletariat.

It has been the usual practice in the class society to keep women politically indifferent, unorganised and, above all, passive, thereby providing a social base for reaction. The social practices and also the media helped to keep the myth of indifference alive. But with the new scientific technological changes, women are no more subservient to their traditional role in the "Kirche, Kiicher and Kinder" (Church, Kitchen and Children). They have started to realise the significance of their contribution in the social development process, a phenomenon, pregnant with consequences for the future.

While the ruling class and increasing sections of the middle class aspire to live up to their ideology, working class women have been involved in organisation and struggle. Even for the privileged sections, from middle and upper classes, the battle lines were drawn for legal equality, access to the professions, to share in the economic and social position of the men of their own class. Many of them even joined, though only temporarily, the struggle for the common cause with working class women over the vote. These class alliances remained only partially effective, since there were basic differences that emerged on issues like the methods to be used in the struggle, for example, on whether the demand should be for universal suffrage or for the property qualification for the vote for men to be extended on the same basis to women.

It was in this period of change that Engels, using the data available to him at that time, tried to show that in the earliest societies, women had not occupied the inferior position allocated to them by capitalism and that their systematic oppression was much more modern. As the title of the book (*The Origin of Family, Private Property and State*) suggests, he linked it to the development of private property, by which he meant the private ownership of the means of production, and the state.

The basic position of Marxism on the biology versus environment debate is that biology obviously plays a role in enabling and restricting what humans can do. But one of the main features of the development of human society is the role played by culture, by technology, knowledge, traditions and ideas. Even if it is the case that the inequality of women is based on the division of labour between men and women in relation to childbearing, there is no reason in modern society why this should continue to be decisive.

The struggle for maternity rights and childcare illustrate the potential for breaking down such a division of labour. It is a social and political decision whether it should be done or not. In his *Theses on Feuerbach,* Marx wrote: "The materialist doctrine that men are products of circumstances and upbringing and that therefore changed men are a product of other circumstances and changed upbringing, forgets that it is men that change circumstances".

In fact the basic power structures perpetuate the rule of class and as part of that class rule, institutions have created a powerful position for men. As a result, the struggle by women against their own oppression tends to converge with the class struggle, against the exploitative system of capitalism that addresses the discrimination and specific oppression of women. It may be pointed out here that women workers were involved in the formation of the earliest trade unions and in struggle.

An important turning-point was the strike of the London match-girls in 1888, when this most exploited and downtrodden section of workers revolted against their oppressors. At the factory in Bow in the poor East End, the workforce was entirely made up of women, from 13-year-old girls to mothers of large families. The barbaric conditions there were similar to those experienced by workers in the Third World now. The use of white phosphorus for making matches produced the dreadful disease which ate away the jaw-bone, as a result of having to eat food in the polluted atmosphere of the workshop. Bad wages were made worse by the iniquitous system of fines, often imposed for the most trivial errors, brought on by fatigue. As a result, the shareholders got a fine dividend of 22 per cent.

Overcoming their fear, in July 1888, 672 of the women struck. In a fortnight, thanks to the support of the trade unions and a public campaign that raised the considerable sum of £400, the women won major concessions. As a result, these unskilled women organised the Matchmakers' Union, the largest union composed of women and girls in England. This was a giant step forward in the explosion of the "New Unionism" in Britain when, for the first time, the unskilled proletariat became organised into unions. This has important lessons for the present period, when, as 100 years ago, a large number of unskilled and semi-skilled workers are unorganised, and a large percentage of these are women.

The Bolsheviks always took the question of revolutionary work among women workers very seriously. Lenin, in particular, attached an enormous importance to this question, especially in the period of the revolutionary upsurge from 1912–14, and during the First World War. It was at this time that International Women's Day (March 8) began to be celebrated with mass workers' demonstrations. It is not an accident that the February 1917 (March, according to the new calendar) revolution arose from disturbances around Women's Day, when women demonstrated against the war and the high cost of living.

However, after the collapse of the Soviet system, the situation has rapidly changed for the worse. The women have been thrown into a position of abject slavery in the hypocritical name of the family. They have to bear the larger share of the burden of the crisis. They are the first to be sacked, in order to avoid paying social benefits, like child and maternity benefit. Given the fact that women made up 51 per cent of the Russian workforce a few years ago, and that 90 per cent of women worked, the growth of unemployment has meant that more than 70 per cent of Russia's unemployed workers are now women. In some areas the figure is 90 per cent.

The difference today is the degree and relative continuity of women's participation in the workforce. Even for those women not in paid employment, their dependence on the pay of working class men has meant a tendency to be involved in spite of the difficulties caused by their role in the family, their isolation in individual households and the prejudice they often encountered in the labour movement, reflecting the ideology promoted by capitalism.

So apart from their involvement in trade unions, they have been involved in support groups and in other formerly mass organisations. The family can no more be abolished than the state. The gradual disappearance of both in the transition to a classless society depends on the transformation of the material conditions of existence of the masses, and therefore, in time, the transformation of the way people think and relate to each other. Eventually, with the achievement of super abundance and a high level of culture, the old habits and slave psychology will be transformed and with it the relations between men and women. But the prior condition for this is a transformation in the conditions of life themselves. One such step could be reduction in the working days. But beyond that, the advances in technology should make possible the virtual abolition of housework: the basis of the domestic slavery of women.

9

Democracy and the Renewal of Socialism

Ishwar Singh Dost

"We are not among those communists who are out to destroy personal liberty, who wish to turn the world into one huge barrack or into a gigantic workhouse. There certainly are some communists who, with an easy conscience, refuse to countenance personal liberty and would like to shuffle it out of the world because they consider that it is a hindrance to complete harmony. But we have no desire to exchange freedom for equality. We are convinced that in no social order will freedom be assured as in a society based on communal ownership." —Karl Marx, 1847 (quoted in Hal Draper, *The Two Souls of Socialism*, available at: http://www.marxists.org/archive/draper/1966/twosouls/3-marx.htm.

Socialism and democracy are mutually related-intrinsically and essentially. There can be no true socialism without democracy, and there can be no real democracy without socialism. The lesson of so-called 'actually existing socialisms' is that socialism cannot be achieved in the absence of democracy. The left should reclaim democracy as an essential socialistic idea. Socialism is the process of self-emancipation of the masses; hence, it cannot be imposed from above.

The limitation of the existing successful model of democracy is that it is confined to the domain of political and social. Capitalism cannot achieve economic democracy that would be the socialisation of mode of production. Socialism should be the radical extension of democracy by applying the same democratic principles to the domain of economic processes. However, in no circumstances should it go back to pre-capitalist, pre-democratic forms of rule as it happened in almost all so-called socialist countries.

20th Century 'Socialism' and Democracy

The biggest failure of the 20th century 'actually existing socialism' or state bureaucratic capitalism was on the issue of democracy. Almost all experiences of building socialism ultimately turned into a state bureaucratic rule, which is the negation of socialist aspirations of self-rule.

Marx's characterisation of the bourgeois state as dictatorship of class should be analysed and debated in the light of historical experience. It seems that Marx's characterisation does not refer to the dictatorship of any particular government, but to the nature of the state, which is the expression of dominant production relations (see Andrew Levine, 1988). History showed that the bourgeois state (and economic relations) generated and developed the mechanism and processes of representation. It gains legitimacy through the operations of constitutional sovereignty, rule of law, human rights, and democratic procedures. A socialist critique may be that there is serious limitation (and class biases) of all the aspects, which should be radicalised and should be made substantive, but the question is not of retreating from the gains of democratic rights.

Marx's Concept of Socialist Democracy

Marx conceived socialist transformation as a revolution against the state. He used the Paris commune as a model of a workers' state, workers' democracy (which is also a starting point of going beyond the state). He insisted that the end of the separation between legislative and executive, the abolition of the standing army, free and universal education, universal suffrage, the right to recall representatives and the limits on the salary of any elected official were all essential elements of any workers' state. The Paris Commune, Marx wrote was 'essentially a working class government... the political form at last discovered under which to work out the economic emancipation of labour'. (Karl Marx, *Civil War in France,* Chapter 3)

There are many examples of replacement of the existing bureaucratic state apparatuses by workers' self-government—the Paris Commune of 1871, workers' and soldiers' councils that assumed power in Russia in October 1917, the Spanish Revolution of 1936–7, the Hungarian Revolution of 1956, Italian workers' council movement, latest workers sector in Spain, Mexico, etc.

Problems

Let us first see the paradox of socialist aspirations and socialist practice. The bourgeois form of class dictatorship also developed the representative, hegemonic and consensual aspects of state power, but the experiences of proletarian class dictatorship put the accent on the repressive, coercive aspects of state power. This is the irony that so-called socialist states do not have the mechanisms of well-defined civil and political rights, rule of law and representative institutions. The question is how the substantive character of democracy and freedom can be achieved without the formal working of institutions and procedures. The left should realise that it fails to conceptualise and evolve alternative political institutions. Apart from all the dreams and rhetoric (to avoid a farcical situation) of the withering away of the state, the left should seriously think how to develop the socialist democratic institutions, procedures and processes of representation, participation and self-rule. It should also consider why there is no adequate Marxist theory of (human) or democratic rights? Why is Marxist jurisprudence so underdeveloped? This is most urgent because of strong vanguardist tendencies of communist culture, which also foster a kind of elitism and majoritarianism. (See Nicholas De Marco's article)

Marx propounded a model of direct democracy as realised in the short-lived Paris Commune. But his theoretical heritage leaves many question unanswered. He criticised and brought to the fore the limitations of bourgeois parliamentary democracy, but did not develop the theory of the future political establishment. David Held points out a major problem with the Marxist conceptualisation: that is the conflict between direct democracy of local autonomous entities and a strong centralised socialist planning. (David Held, 1997, p. 147) Now there are some theoretical discussions and experiments of decentralised planning going on, but all these cannot solve the problem of coordination. The problem is how the local organisations of direct democracy can be associated with each other. For this, do we require some institution of representative democracy—open and accountable institutions at state or national level?

A viable model of socialist democracy can be built based on direct democracy and local autonomy, but it has to incorporate some elements from the model of representative (parliamentary) democracy (multiparty democracy). Participatory democracy at the every sphere of social activity would be its foundation. Power is as far as possible decentralised. New institutions and procedures have to be laid down and built for this purpose like the self-managing federation of workers, consumers, and neighbourhood councils. Can there be a system of democratic planning through which decisions about the allocation of resources were collectively taken. Here a mix of direct democracy and representative democracy can be developed.

Political democracy also entails democratic culture and right to information and free expressions. It will be based on free access to information and the ability to take part in public discussion. The communist parties have to alter their organisational principles like democratic centralism for achieving this. It is also necessary because this question cannot be left to the whims (or goodness) of leaders, but proper, procedural constitutional details should be developed.

References

Javed Alam, 'Beyond Enlightenment: Democratising Modernity', a paper presented at a seminar organised by Alam Khundmiri Foundation, Hyderabad, January 10–12, 2008.

Alex Callinicos, 'Socialism: Political Vision', www.zmag.org/ callinicospol.htm.

David Held, *Models of Democracy*, Polity Press, Cambridge, 1997.

Andrew Levine, *Arguing for Socialism: Theoretical Considerations*, Verso, London, 1988.

Nicholas De Marco, 'Marxism and Democracy: Apex and Abrogation', *UCL Jurisprudence Review*, 2000.

Karl Marx, Civil War in France available at www.marxists.org/archive/marx/works/1871/civil-war-france/index. htm - 4k.

10

21st Century Socialism

Khagendra Thakur

What is the Basic Feature of the 21st Century?

It is the continuation of the last phase of the 20th century.

It is being called the post Soviet Era, Post Cold War Era, Information Age, Age of Science and Technology and finally Age of Globalisation.

All these expressions are to cover the basic features of this period. Basically it is the phase of the new type of imperialism, i.e. domination of finance capital—dictatorship of finance capital over the world.

Its main contradiction—socialism was relevant not because of the October Revolution, not because of Marxism, but because of the exploitative character of capitalism. Is capitalism exploitation free or contradiction free today?

Socialism is relevant today for the victims of capitalism, may it be the underdeveloped nations or poor and working people inside a country. But exploitation does not work for social transformation automatically.

People are to be organised and prepared for fighting for the social justice transformation. Objective conditions exist, but subjective forces are not strong enough to exploit the situation.

Capitalism is strong due to the protection of the governments protecting capitalism in the fields of economy, finance, politics and ideology.

As a social system, capitalism's weakness may be experienced in the market. A vast majority of people are pushed out of the market. These people can be organised as a fighting force against capitalism and for socialism. People's concern for humane culture and democracy may be undertaken up to attract people in fighting capitalism.

Obstructions in Socialist Transformation of Indian Society

1. Specifics of Indian society today—nature and class character of this society. Multistructural nature confuses the class character.
2. Theory of main contradiction vs the main enemy in politics.
3. Character of Indian democracy. Parliamentary system vs revolutionary transformation of the society.
4. Indian communist movement and parliamentary system.
5. Parliamentary and people's revolutionary movement. Movement led by T.U. Kisan Sabha and agricultural labour—their limitations.
6. Relief measures sponsored by the government and their scope. Attitude of the mass organisations towards these measures.
7. Relief measures vs revolutionary change in society.
8. Ideas that grip the minds of the people in India.
9. Main ideological obstacles before socialist ideas in Indian society.

10. Failure of the communist movement in convincing people that socialism and socialist transformation of society is part of the Indian tradition.
11. Failure of communist movement in taking working class with its historic task. Failure in using the contradictions between capitalism and the working class in India.
12. Attitude towards casteism and communalism in Indian society, deideolisation and depoliticisation.
13. Failure in presenting unity of words and deeds.
14. Failure in making the communist movement a growing political force.
15. Failure in convincing people that their problems have been created by capitalism, hence it is unable to solve their problems.
16. Trying to take advantage of capitalism on one hand and fighting against it on the other—cannot go together.

11

Globalisation and Prospect of Socialism in the 21st Century

Bhanudeb Dutta

Introduction

The Soviet Union's collapse led many scholars of different countries, including ours, to think in line with the bourgeois ideologue Fukuyama's "end of history." This colossal incident made them express gleefully that Marxism was nothing but utopianism. By expressing such continuous whimper, they themselves open up their mind that the phenomenon is temporary. They cannot even forget that Marx was adjudged as "Millennium Greatest Thinker "by a poll organised by BBC and Reuters. Marx was such a great scholar and thinker that he along with his lifelong comrade Engels, could foresee the internal dynamics of capitalism and its development through searching for its market beyond its own country which we in the present day call 'globalisation'.

It is to be admitted without any doubt that globalisation, that we talk much about now, is an objective trend in the process of capitalism's journey. It is the historical stage of the development of capitalism.

Two Aspects of Capitalism in the Globalisation Process

That capitalism will attain such a stage was indicated vividly in the *Communist Manifesto* of Marx-Engels in 1848. They indicated the globalising characteristics of capitalism. They gave an idea of the intention of the bourgeois towards extensively and constantly increasing the productive forces by constantly revolutionising the instruments of production and with them the whole relations of society. In *Capital* Vol. 1, in Chapter 32, on the subject 'Historical Tendency of Capitalist Accumulation', Marx depicted the destructive role of the bourgeoisie.

They depicted the bourgeois motive for amassing inhuman profit through coercion, repression and blood sucking of the working people. This tendency relates to another aspect of capitalism, i.e. production relations. While judging capitalism one cannot and should not concentrate only on building the productive forces by closing their eyes to production relations. There two components are organically linked to any production system and capitalism is no exception to it. We should study these two aspects dialectically in the present-day capitalist globalisation.

Dialectics of Globalisation

In the last century capitalism underwent a number of stages, e.g. privately owned monopoly, state monopoly and transnational monopoly. Capitalism is now transnational with global integration. The aim of capitalism is to establish "Full Spectrum Dominance "over the entire globe in all areas and sectors projecting a universal system. This is the strategy of the New Century American Project. Globalisation is nothing but global economic expansion by MNC/TNC through liberalisation and privatisation with new dispensation of market economy, neoliberal policy, regime change policy, economic and ecological onslaught, consumerism, etc. Capitalism tries to force its unhindered advance through these. This is one side of capitalism.

There is another side. It cannot eliminate the inherent contradiction of capitalism. Illusion of "new capitalism", assertion of "End of History" and baseless conclusion of TINA—have all been shattered to pieces. More and more scholars, historians and intellectuals now forcefully voice their protest against the failure of economic globalisation. Leave aside speaking of developing a nation through globalisation, it is actually aimed at destroying these through IMF, WB and WTO.

We can recall here the four-point formula of globalisation as exposed by Joseph Stiglitz, former Chief of the World Bank. These formula serve the agenda of rich nations, pressure 'client countries' and beneficiaries to adopt privatisation which meant actually briberisation, Capital market liberalisation meaning hot money cycle, market-based pricing meaning IMF riot and free trade meant as China's opium war. The emerging crises arising out of the above are incompatibility between the monetary system and actual economic system, crises and recession in the world economy like 1930's speculative activities, etc.

These facts go to prove that the contradiction of capitalism cannot be solved within the framework of capitalism itself. This means that the inherent contradiction in the capitalist mode of production remains but gets further sharpened. The contradiction between pervasive dimension of socialisation of productive forces especially in the wake of STR and private ownership in the relations of production exist as usual. The incapacity to correct this contradiction is congenital to the different stages of capitalism inclusive of the stage of economic globalisation.

The contradictions arise from the existence of four contradictions in manifold aggravated form as enumerated by the communist movement long ago. Here one can say that in the absence of the Soviet Union, how can the contradiction between imperialism and socialism become the main one? In fact, the main contradiction is not identified between two states but between two different ideologically-based social systems, may be emerging, existing or extinct.

Prospects of Socialism in the 21st Century

The "Brains" of the US-Republican Party in September 2000 drafted a document for "Rebuilding American's Defences'. After Bush won the election and became the US-President for the first time, that draft was given an official seal under the title "Project New American Century" (PNAC). It is easily understandable that they think that the 21st century will be the US-century. In April, 2005, China's Prime Minister Wen Ziabao while addressing the students of the Indian Institute of Technology in Delhi observed that the 21st century will be the century of Asia. Venezuelan President Hugo Chavez said in pride at Kolkata at a public reception meeting that this century will be that of Asia, Africa and Latin American countries. The Communist Party of India in its Political Resolution adopted in January 2005 asserted, "There is a gradual shift in the power centre from West to the East. The 21st century should become Asia's century."

Who can deny that even after the Soviet Union's collapse, that Marxism is still the much talked about ideology by either the adherents or adversaries? Cuba, China and Vietnam still exist with socialism as their aim. Moreover, the different socialist or people's revolutions have been able to demonstrate that capitalism can be overthrown and a new and higher system like socialism can be built. Profound changes have taken place in many Latin American countries replacing the US-pampered governments by left democratic forces. There is an upsurge of the anti-globalisation movement, anti-war movement, World Social Forum's gathering, Save Ecology movement, etc. in every corner of the world. The Communists' meet, e.g. in Athens, Lisbon, Byelorussia, etc. at international seminars and conferences point out the focus on the "globalisation and global aggressive nature of US-imperialism". These are all positive developments. Within all these anti-imperialist and anti-capitalist movements, seeds of socialism exist although many participate without any knowledge of it. The duty of the communists is to give it a proper direction with a clear perspective.

The emergence of a multipolar world, the constant surfacing of inter imperialist contradiction, the formation of ASEAN, Latin American Block, Shanghai Cooperation organisation, SAFTA, LAFTA, NAASP, Indo-Russia-China Friendly Axis, economic scandals in capitalist countries, deep depression in many G-8 countries, disillusionment for the neoliberal policies beginning to be felt in many developing countries are all positive developments. In this connection, a word of caution should be given to the UPA Government of India that they are blind to see these developments. Instead they plunged the country into a deep agricultural crisis and opened the floodgates for MNCs to establish corporate capitalism. However, on a global scale, during the last few years we find the emergence of socialist thought and movement. These prove the setbacks are not evidence to the failure of Marxism nor show that Marx's basic Ideas on capitalism and socialism are outmoded.

Capitalism in the globalisation process though takes advantage of STR for averting the crisis and prolonging its existence, it creates full material and social preconditions for its inevitable doom. This happens independent of the will of the bourgeoisie because it is an objective trend of development. This is the dialectics of capitalism. In the words of Lenin, we can say that "Socialism is now gasing at us from all the windows of modern capitalism." So the economic globalisation shall expedite the course of historical process for the replacement of capitalism by a higher form of social system and that is by socialism. I firmly believe in the irreversibility of the replacement of capitalism by socialism, if judged against the long history of social development.

A Word of Caution for Future Socialism

There was conceptual misunderstanding for socialism in the past. At whatever stage of revolution we remain, we actually live in a society, which in Marx's language is called civil society. In this society, many civil types of political and social contradiction exist, which needs to be solved to arrive at socialism. In the solution of all these, the movement needs to be broadly expanded. Apart from addressing the political issues, social issues need to be addressed. The movement needs to take a political—civil character instead of state (government)—political character. People need to be helped to take a class-based initiative rather than government-based initiative. Gramsci emphasised in his *Prison Notebook* to win the people not by 'domination' 'but by 'intellectual and moral leadership'.

Secondly, at the stage of socialism, two types of tendencies exist side by side. It is not a permanent system. It is not a system without contradiction or without problems. Within socialism, features of civil society do not end and that of human society, which Marx called for communist society, begin to sprout. So at the stage of socialism, struggle against these goes on. Thirdly, in the process of negating capitalism, we arrive at socialism. As the productive force of capitalism creates the objective basis of socialism, constant struggle for conversion of production-relations in our favour will go on and the struggle should go on against the discriminatory features in the superstructure. Otherwise the transition to socialism will be faulty. This means that in capitalism the class and democratic struggle will go hand in hand. It also means that class organisation and mass organisations should be strengthened simultaneously.

Fourthly, in a country like ours, some features of pre-capitalist formation still exist, e.g. religious fundamentalism, caste system, communalism, etc. Moreover multi-lingual, multi-cultural, multi-religious, multi-socio-economic formation of our country should be considered while formulating strategy and tactics of democratic revolution with an orientation towards socialism.

Fifthly, can we not with our own expertise in all fields restrict the inflow of foreign capital when we know that it ultimately amounts to surrender to international monopoly capital? Proper planning and domestic resource mobilisation will have to be emphasised.

Sixthly, the classical form of the working class is at present changed. But the overall working class is growing in size. Apart from the manufacturing sector, they come from the service sector, knowledge sector, unorganised sector, etc. Even the unemployed employable persons and persons thrown out of employment come within the ambit of working class. Everybody in these sectors are victims of appropriation of surplus-value by the owners of the means of production, business magnets, entrepreneurs, etc.

So all come within the framework of working class. From the mid-20th century bio-technology, information technology, microelectronics, etc. play an important role in the development of society. The socialist movement must take care of this development and ponder over devising new forms of movement with the new working class along with the classical form of working class.

Lastly, in the domain of struggle between capital and labour, not only the organised working class but also the unorganised subaltern people like Dalits, Adivasis and agricultural workers should be involved. Considering all these, we can say that the 21st century will not be the US-century, but the end of the US-century with the triumph of socialism.

12

Socialism in the 21st Century

Ram Narsimha Rao

Socialism is an inevitable social system crossing the stage of capitalism. Historical materialism is a doctrine which substantiates that socialism is a socio-economic system which has to be passed prior to reaching the stage of communism. Socialism in the erstwhile Soviet Union could achieve several victories in various walks of life. It was about to reach an advanced stage of socialism where development was glaringly visible in many fields like space research, Olympics, heavy industry, medicine, etc. It could survive on its own without anyone's support and subsequently it has stood just like a rock behind the socialist block of countries and also gave maximum aid to national liberation movements and also gave its fullest cooperation in establishing public sector heavy industries in the underdeveloped countries.

It was not the failure of socialism as a system, but its managers had failed in managing that system by not understanding it properly; there were three major factors for the failure of socialism in the Soviet Union. Firstly, the Soviet Union had to invest a huge amount on defence and also for the protection of the socialist block. Secondly, thousands of younger people were on the frontline for several years, far from their native places. Once they had come back en-block, they could not be provided employment and discontent arose. Thirdly, the Soviet Union could not use the fruits of the scientific and technological revolution properly. While assessing socialism, let us not look at the issues in isolation, but in relation to the track record of capitalism.

An important point to note is that capitalism cannot exist and develop without constantly expanding its sphere of dominance, without colonising new countries and drawing the old non-capitalist countries into the whirlpool of the world economy.

It is more than obvious that state regulation of capitalist economy is ineffective. The measures the bourgeois governments take against inflation foster stagnation of production and growth of unemployment, in the effort to contain the critical drop in production, which lends greater and still greater momentum to inflation.

Capitalist methods and forms of economic association of the different countries leads to consolidation of the division of the world into the centre and peripheral/economically backward agrarian and primary commodity producing countries exploited by them.

Lenin rightly predicted in those days that economic "annexation" is fully achievable without political annexation and is widely practised today. A country may appear to be free and independent, if you consult geography or an atlas. But if you look behind, you find that it is in the grip of another country, or rather its bankers and businessmen.

In the lifetime of Marx and Engels, communism was no more than a vision. It was Marx who in his immortal work, *Capital* transformed socialism, once a Utopia, into a science and demonstrated in theory that the advent of the communist formation is inevitable.

Marxism is not only a theoretical expression of the interests of the working class, but also a summing up of the advances made in the social and natural sciences in the course of mankind's spiritual development. The bourgeoisie claim that capitalism had brought economic prosperity with the advent of mass production and consequently the availability of cheap mass produced goods to the working masses.

But after the collapse of the Soviet Union which mainly concentrated on heavy industry, space research and defending the socialist block, China has appeared on the scene and is dominating the world market. At present, the US market is dumped with Chinese consumer goods. Their pharmaceuticals and chemicals are dumped on to many developing countries. As Marx visualised, abundance of products is possible in developed socialism. This is shown in practice by China.

Soviet socialism could not use the achievements of the Scientific and Technological Revolution, whereas China has adopted the policy of interdependency of both systems and could develop in various fields.

Though China has invited multinationals with foreign investments, it had effectively limited their power so that they do not interfere in political affairs or internal matters. China is using its own enormous manpower and also its achievements in STR, and expanding its market to several nations. Moreover, it is not investing a substantial budget on military as America is investing on its expansionist policies. So socialism in China will advance in its own way.

In Russia also, the administrators cannot go towards capitalism; neither can they make it a colony of another country. The Russian Federation is a mighty country and it has to advance in its own way, rectifying its mistakes. But a tremendous positive factor is the coming together of Russia and China, which has made the US feel insecure. We have confidence that socialism will triumph once again and the advance towards communism is inevitable.

13

Impact of Neoliberal Globalisation on the Working Class

H. Mahadevan

The ever advancing technology has made the working class in the traditional sense mostly redundant, otiose and obsolete. New technology which may eliminate the use of labour and inflict unemployment cannot he resisted. Mechanisation of agriculture and all forms of agribusiness, agrarian labour and rural employment may be gravely jeopardised. Small-scale industries and cooperatives, even tiny industries, face crisis unable to withstand competition from gargantuan globalisation. Labour, i.e. the working class, will vanish if globalisation rolls on at full speed. The few who survive will be well paid and many given a golden handshake. Our constitutional social justice promise will be fading footnotes in the history of the coming century. This is the 'Future Shock.'

How will the Flexibilisation Affect Labour?

Some of the flexibilisation measures identified by the ILO, have been intensified in use in the 1990s. These are:

1. Reducing the core of permanent workers, while increasing the proportion of temporary and casual employees.
2. Increasing the use of women, apprentices and migrants.

3. Subcontracting the production of components previously manufactured within the factory.
4. Subcontracting services like transport, packaging, maintenance and security which were traditionally carried out on factory premises.
5. Increasing the number of shifts per day or the use of overtime.
6. Replacing pay systems based on working time and length of service by systems based on piece rates and (productivity linked) payments or bonuses.
7. Introducing internal training systems which facilitate re-deployment of workers within the factory or enterprise.
8. Reducing influences from 'external' trade union organisations by either eliminating unions or establishing a 'controllable' union.

Central to the flexibilisation process is the ability of companies to "reengineer" themselves by concentrating on core or flagship businesses and spinning off non-core businesses through subcontracting or outsourcing. Strong unions do exist in segments of the service sector like banking, insurance, etc. However, the modern segments such as IT and IT enabled services (ITES), retail outlets (shopping malls) present formidable challenges. Trade unions will have to continue to wage social struggles against powerful economic entities like the TNCs. Large factories offer economies of scale for organising workers. Their organisational system involves organising people employed on wage contract, building employment contracts, negotiation with visible employers, institutional separation of negotiable issues and non-negotiable issues, and mobilising and striking against specific (employers). But these characteristics are not prevalent in most cases in the informal sector.

Universal Human Rights and Socialism

The essence of universal human happiness is distributive justice, based on sharing and caring, on human rights as everyone's right to life in dignity free from hunger, illiteracy and denial of equal opportunity and status. Even here, the law and life must go together and if life is to be human, not savage. Many Asian countries are home to the largest number of the world's poor and destitute, illiterate and shelterless humans, victims of infant mortality and maternal mortality. As per the Directive Principles of State Policy, the state shall in particular, direct its policy towards securing:

(a) That the citizens, men and women equally have the right to an adequate means of livelihood.

(b) That the ownership and control of the community are so distributed as best to subserve the common good.

(c) That the operation of the economic system does not result in the concentration of wealth and means of production to the common detriment.

These are becoming irrelevant in the globalised capital intensive market economy.

Resistance that Opens Up Possibilities

In many countries of the developing world the workers and people oppose the solutions that the multinationals, big powers and their institutions wish to impose. The WTO talks, especially those on the General Agreement on Trade and Services (GATS), are in difficulties, and the battle to cancel Third World debt is gaining ground. In Latin America, the people are struggling against the Free Trade Agreements for the Americas (ALCA) and the Free Trade Agreements (FTAs), which are neo-colonialist tools that the USA is trying to impose.

Countries are deciding to take control of their resources to the advantage of their own people and are establishing superior social programmes as part of the non-capitalist way of development. Interesting ideas are being experimented with; ideas that are far removed from IMF doctrine—micro-credit cooperatives focusing around the need for jobs, reorganisation of agriculture to meet internal needs, South-South cooperation on mutually beneficial terms, etc. In the developed countries numerous campaigns demand an end to job insecurity and solidarity is being organised to ensure that migrant workers irrespective of their situation, are treated properly and receive the same industrial and social rights as local workers. At this time the various forms of opposition, experiences and struggles have not yet succeeded in reversing the neoliberal offensive but they have opened up valuable possibilities.

Workers always resist the power of capital in one way or the other and the last few years/decades have been no exception. Some exciting events took place during the 1990s. The labour made common cause with the various strands of the anti-globalisation movement, most notably in Seattle, Cancun, amongst others. In same countries labour also allied itself with the growing student-centred anti-sweatshop movement. In poorer countries, protests against the devastation brought by neoliberalism were widespread.

In Mexico, the Zapatistas began their struggle for peasant self-rule, the very day the North American Free Trade Agreement went into effect. In Brazil, a movement of landless peasants combined with a National Workers' Party not only to liberate land for the landless but also to propel Lula de Silva into the country's highest political office and they were benefited. The workers and toiling people of Venezuela defended the Government of Hugo Chavez against the American-inspired capitalist offensive to overthrow the democratically elected government As a part of the global struggle against market economy the massive demonstrations organised by the working people of Europe along with the progressive social movements faced severe repression.

Some changes in the ruling political set up were contributed on account of the toiling people and working class actions in India, though the supporting parties of the workers could not capture power. The struggle against the monarchy in Nepal, also participated by the working class in a big way, finally met with success for the democratic forces and the struggle for economic freedom still continues. While all these diverse actions and movements were important movements and each managed to achieve some improvements for workers and their duties, rather individually, did they mark a turning point in the class struggles? Union defensives have continued to the fall and depredations of neoliberalism have continued unabated. US imperialism has become mare nakedly aggressive, using September 11, 2001 as cover for military mayhem and further assaults on workers' rights and security in the US itself.

A common struggle of all workers becomes necessary in alliance with the peasants and rural people, in order to achieve democratic and progressive agrarian reforms that might place the land in the hands of those who toil. Our trade unions both internationally and nationally, should be the framework for the younger generations, immigrant workers, the unemployed the dispossessed of rights, those excluded from the collective bargaining to organise and defend themselves, in particular the millions of workers, men and women in the informal sector. Trade unions have a decisive role, along with their allies, to put an end to these anti-working class and also in many cases anti-national policies.

Discussion and Conclusion

The main subject of the symposium-cum-workshop "Socialism in the 21st Century" was divided into 8 (eight) topics.

1. Socialism in the 21st century
2. Problems of building socialism in the 20th century
3. Marxism and modern science and technology
4. Socialism and democracy—issues of decentralisation and empowerment
5. India's path to socialism
6. Socialism and the market and the role of planning
7. The changing nature of work and role of labour
8. Socialist Knowledge Society

The discussion or the base paper prepared by Anil Rajimwale covered these topics, and provided a basis for discussion. M. Vijaya Kumar also presented a comprehensive paper. The 13 papers presented by the participants covered various aspects of the themes or the topics. There were wide ranging and very enriching discussions over three days by the participants. They focused on several aspects, which used in-depth as well as extensive discussions, debates and studies/analyses.

Among the participants, A.B. Bardhan and S. Sudhakar Reddy in their speeches in the inaugural sessions presented before many questions and problems related with the aspects of the present political situation and of the political programme. A.B. Bardhan emphasised the need to evolve India's own path to socialism. S. Sudhakar Reddy suggests that the masses themselves need socialism.

Changes in Capitalism and the Need for a Programme

It was felt that capitalism in India as well as the world over had entered a new phase of development. It was becoming more modern, corporatisation was proceeding apace, real estate was growing rapidly, the stock exchange mechanism was on the rise, and finance capital was growing. The MNCs were gaining ground. Liberalisation and globalisation were among the new features.

At the same time, it was observed that it would be a one-sided approach to only emphasise the growth of big business. Small and medium production, business and capitalism was, at the same time, not only growing but also asserting themselves.

The concept of the non-capitalist path had to be given up in this context, although some felt that it will have to be anti-capitalist, anti-neoliberal path of development, initiating suspension of several capitalist laws. In the analysis and characterisation of capitalism, it was essential to deeply study the STR (scientific and technological revolution) and the ICR (information and communication revolution).

It would be a mistake to look for a 'comprador' section in the Indian bourgeoisie in its present stage. Comprador bourgeoisie was mainly a phenomenon of China, and also to an extent of the early stages of Indian capitalism. Comprador is a section that is mainly a trading one, depending on the export-import trade with the foreign bourgeoisie. Its interest in productive industry, if any, is only secondary.

Today, the Indian capitalist class and its various sections have evolved into a powerful productive force, as well as financial, trading, commercial and other kinds. It has its own independent base and role. It is not parasitic. It does compromise with imperialism and finance capital, but not as parasites, but on the basis of their own strength and in their own interest.

Lately, belief in socialism has strengthened. A number of events within the country and the world over have helped people to regain confidence and enthusiasm, e.g. the left-supported UPA government in India, installation of left-leaning governments in Latin America through elections. Prolonged phase or phases of democratic transformations would be needed before conditions for socialism are created.

Need for Broad-Based Outlook

A rigid, sectarian outlook and approach has to be given up. We should not adopt a hostile attitude to religion and spiritualism. Some participants related their experience and results of their study. They were studying Swamy Vivekananda and others. Their heritage should be carried forward. Spiritualism among the people inculcated many positive tendencies and outlook in the cultural and humanist field. And this should not be ignored.

Indian reality is a complex and complicated one. All the democratic forces should come together on people's issues, and find common bases. Yet some have tried to create divisions.

More than political party alliances, it is the alliance of political classes that is needed. The class approach has to be followed. Reforms have vector quality and quantity: they have certain paradigms, directions and implications. Therefore, they need proper thinking. While welcoming Venezuelan and Latin American events, let us not go ga-ga over them. Let us coolly assimilate their experiences. They are facing many difficulties. Let us study their actual policies. There is no working class of the old type in these countries. Chavez was a Trotskyite. He is trying to do many things. There is a silver lining to the defeat of the Referendum. That has put a halt to the authoritarian tendencies and to the habit of ruling by decree. After all, it is a democratic system, which should be strengthened. That is also the lesson of the failed socialist models. You cannot bring socialism suddenly on a whim.

Workers across castes have to be united; it has to be class unity inclusive of struggle against casteism and for social justice. The caste problem cannot be solved automatically. In India, the downtrodden castes have to face the wrath of imperialism as well.

Today, a prolonged process of democratic transformations is the essence of the main struggles. Today, society has become very complicated, multi-sided and multi-layered. STR is adding new dimensions.

There are several questions that need to be tackled in the context of socialism, e.g. market, capitalist relations, democracy, etc. Lenin realised the need to tackle them after revolution, if socialism was to be built successfully. He realised the need for the productive forces to be developed. Therefore, he formulated the New Economic Policy (NEP), as a necessary condition to develop socialism in Russia. But Stalin scuttled it and adopted the path of forced collectivisation and industrialisation at the cost of the peasantry, with the help of a vast repressive machinery. Democratic practices were violated and whatever existing democratic institutions were destroyed. These acts and crimes against party and people were sought to be justified using the pretext of the fascist threat and the Second World War. But actually repressions started much earlier, immediately after Lenin's death. After all, Lenin also led the struggle against intervention by 14 imperialist countries and civil war, and when there was only a nebulous Red Army. Yes, imperialist invasion was defeated by a collective leadership led by Lenin and without sepression of any party leaders and cadres.

Socialism as a Stage of Social Development

There were interesting discussions on the nature of socialism as a stage of social development. It has to be clearly realised that socialism should be dealt as a distinct socio-economic formation, as the next stage of social development after capitalism. As such, several problems of socialism or socialist-orientation cannot be dealt with subjectively and in terms of the wishes of leaders alone.

According to the laws of historical materialism, each proceeding socio-economic formation (relations of production) creates better and more favourable conditions for growth of the productive forms. Though the productive forces developed considerably in the former Soviet Union and Eastern Europe, and though at certain stages in certain areas, the Soviet Union forged ahead of the USA and the West (Sputnik, rocketing, areas of defence), it began to lag behind rapidly from the 1970s onwards. Electronics, computer revolution, STR and ICR more or less bypassed the socialist countries.

This was because the new technology did not become a social force, and remained confined to and closed in certain pockets controlled by the state. That is how the state and bureaucracy became a hurdle in the path of the development of the productive forces.

In this context, the questions of democracy in relation to socialism become crucial. What are the checks and balances of the social system over its leaders, bureaucracy and political parties? How do you decide what particular step is to be taken and when? What is the legal-constitutional validity of the ruling party? Why were there no rights to open press, organisations, mass movements, freedom of expression, etc? Why were labour-industrial laws violated and continue to be violated in the countries ruled by the CPs? How does the policy of 'hire and fire' and deprivation of TU rights square up with the socialist system?

So, in essence did a system as such ever evolve in these countries in favour of and by the working class?

What is then a ruling working class or a rule by and a system of the working class? Here the observations and warnings of Rosa Luxemburg appear quite relevant. She pointed out that the Soviet rule was a rule on behalf of the workers rather than by the workers themselves. Later, during Stalin's period whatever existing democratic functioning was thrown to the winds. The country came to be ruled not even by the party, but by a coterie headed by Stalin, in reality by him alone with the help of the intelligence department and the army. Maoism is another variety of Stalinism.

This of course does not take away the positive contributions of Stalin and Mao, particularly during the Second World War by the former. A balanced assessment of Stalin should be made. Yet he and Mao should not be excused for their mistakes and crimes, not in order to vilify them, but to learn from history.

Yet, the problem remains that the events in the socialist countries are sought to be explained through the wishes of this or that leader, and not through the working of the system. A socio-economic system, a new stage in the social development cannot collapse just at the will or doings of one person (e.g. 'Gorbachev destroyed the Soviet Union', etc.). And if it collapses at the will and wish of one person, then it is not a socialist system, not a social system at all. Can feudalism or capitalism collapse at the wish of one person?

Therefore, we have to go deeper into the reasons and roots of the events in the Soviet Union and Eastern Europe. Some day, it is just a model that has collapsed, not socialism. But the question is far more complicated than this. Earlier no one talked of a 'model'; it was simply stated that it was socialism.

Imperialist circles declared Marxism and socialism dead. But the movement is still alive, and not just alive but more active. China and other countries are trying to chart out new paths to socialism, according to many participants. It is challenging the USA in many areas.

Yet there were many disturbing trends in China, which raise basic issues in the context of socialism. The number of billionaires is growing, unemployment is on the rise, the gap between the rich and poor is increasing, capitalists and MNCs are being given a free hand, the state sector has already lost its commanding heights, 'LPG' is on a roll, privatisation is spreading like a cancer, and so on. Has China taken a full-fledged capitalist path?

There is no doubt that China needs modern productive forces and growth, and that is welcome. But is it not being done at the cost of production relations?

These and other questions need to be analysed. While welcoming certain aspects of the development in China, one need not commit oneself to its claims for 'socialism', and thus not commit the same mistakes as in the case of other socialist countries. Some participants noted that China was using the market just as a tool and not as forces. Market and commodity production were tools. So, there is no such thing as 'market socialism'. Socialism was a long process. Others differed, who commented that China, in fact, was building a huge market, which was going out of control. Market forces were in full play, and China would be swamped by them. China tried its best to enter into the WTO, while we opposed entry for India into the WTO tooth and nail.

Technological Determinism

Some participants criticised Anil Rajimwale's base paper as an example of technological determinism. Istvan Meszaros was quoted to say that technology is class-oriented. Nano-technology for whom? It was asked. People do not even get food, what will they do with 'nano-tech'? Is nano needed for socialism?

Gender and Socialism

Krishna Jha's paper caused a heated debate on the gender question in general, and on the relationship between the gender question and socialism. Even socialism had ignored the gender question as to be solved automatically with the solution of the class question. While feminism was incorrect in its criticism of Marxism, there were many gaps in the latter. The socialist/communist and Marxist movement still suffer from dilemmas and double-dealing, and enough theoretical and practical work has not been done. The structure of the CPs and lack of women's representation in them bear witness to these facts.

Changing Structure of the Working Class

There was an interesting discussion on the changing structure of the working class. The STR had brought about qualitative changes in the means of production and communications. Besides, several transformations had taken place in the world economy. Consequently, the old working class, of which Marx talked about, has almost gone. The new workers have much to lose.

Besides, there is a rapid shift in the workers from production to information and knowledge. Knowledge workers are becoming the bigger proportion of the working class.

These changes pose new problems of approach, demands, organisation and perspectives, as well as of the bases of the revolutionary movement.

Caste, Class and the Indian realities

New realities are emerging in India. The study of the character of Indian society till now has been far from satisfactory.

It has to be realised, as an unfortunate fact, that socialism is not part of Indian society and psyche, while religion or caste consciousness are part of it. That only means that socialism has to be inculcated.

What is the class character of communalism? This question has not been answered; it has been evaded. Also, what was the character of Janata Dal? The working class party is weak in its own class.

New realities of tribals, who are changing: some richer sections, some educated, urbanised. Tribes are changing, in transition. Tribals have many forms of existence. According to some participants, therefore, the non-capitalist path of development was still valid.

Importance of Reforms

One way or the other, various parties including the leftist ones are practising reforms. Therefore, they need to be theorised. Today, reforms are a powerful tool, which cannot be fitted into the old style concept of revolution.

So, clear theoretical orientation and work are needed. RTI and NREGS are examples as powerful tools. Knowledge and empowerment of the people would play a more important role in future.

Theoretical Sources

The participants emphasised the need to study the works of other Marxist and non-Marxist thinkers, besides Marx, Engels and Lenin, to enrich Marxist theory. Thinkers like Rosa Luxemburg, Antonio Gramsci, Trotsky, Lukacs, Kautsky, Bukharin, Togliatti, Habermas, Tofflev, Foucault, those of the Frankfurt School, and many others have contributed extensively and pointed to and developed several aspects of contemporary theory.

In this context, a critical study and assimilation, and critical assessment of post-modernism and various critical theories are necessary. A host of 'post' theories have evolved, which have made their own contributions to theory. While many of their aspects are to be critically examined and criticised, many others should be welcomed. Both ways, their contributions should be recognised and assimilated.

Post-modernism is an important field of study. The post-Second World War developments in philosophy, particularly linguistic philosophy, cultural studies, sociology and economics, emergence of the world market and its impact on theory, the communication revolution and its impact on thought-process and formation of consciousness, and so on are bringing about fundamental changes in the nature and structure of thought and theory.

While it is essential to defend the basic formulations and theories of Marxism, and their relevance, in the face of the imperialist offensive, it is at the same time necessary to assimilate everything that is new in theory and practice, so as to keep developing Marxist theory. Marxism, after all, is not a dogma but a science and a guide to actions.

Marxism as Frontier Thinking

Marxism is at the very frontier of thought, the leading edge and the most advanced. It has been so since Marx, who studied and assimilated the latest in every field of his times—from natural sciences, philosophy, economics, social sciences and revolution and forms of it. There is every reason to believe/that it will continue to be frontier thought.

One should keep updating the scientific theory; otherwise it will fall behind the times. Therefore, the latest developments in all the fields should be studied and assimilated.

STR, ICR and the Role of Knowledge

There were very fruitful, interesting and in-depth discussions on the STR, ICR and the role of knowledge/ information in the present and the future societies. In fact, socialism was discussed in the context of these developments, and it was found that the future socialism would be different in many ways.

The papers presented, in particular, by Anil Rajimwale and M. Vijaya Kumar, provided the platform for these discussions. The STR was not only of equal importance as the industrial revolution of the 18th century but even more important. The communication revolution resulting from it has contributed knowledge as a crucial factor.

STR and ICR have changed many paradigms and added new facets. From the practical revolutionary point of view, they are making a deep impact on the nature and composition of society and classes, state, market, parties, media, forms/methods of struggles and revolution, etc. For example, the composition of society is changing in the direction of urbanisation, making it necessary to reorient the revolutionary movement. Peasants/farmers and productive workers are receding in history. The broad middle strata are growing. Role of knowledge, information and media has increased as never before.

These developments also pose the problem of the bases of the left and communist movement.

New means of production and communication are emerging, with great significance for the future socialism, particularly in the context of the ownership pattern. A socialism of the future will have to base itself increasingly on the production and distribution of knowledge/information, and thus will have several new features. All these have to be worked out.

Stagnation in the International Working Class Movement

There has been confusion and stagnation in the international working class movement after the fall of the Soviet and other regimes. One of the reasons has been the ideological confusion. Therefore, ideological-theoretical confusion has to be cleared and a lot of work is necessary in this direction. Study of the changes in the contemporary world and developing Marxism in their light is part of the process.

Events in Latin America, Europe and elsewhere have given immense hope. One can even say that US imperialism is not having its sway on all the issues, and is even getting isolated on many points.

Nature of the Russian Revolution

There was animated discussion on the nature, subsequent development and lessons of the Russian Revolution. Questions of violation of democracy and socialist legality, and of Stalinist repressions also came up. It was suggested that there could be no real socialism without democratic rights to the people.

Future socialism has to learn many lessons from the collapse of centralised bureaucratic regimes in East Europe and the Soviet Union.

Socialism and Knowledge

M. Vijaya Kumar's paper advanced the concept of Socialist Knowledge Society. Knowledge would play a decisive role in the future socialism. Many features would change accordingly, including the use of knowledge and ownership question.

Computers are secondary, human beings are primary. We cannot go beyond the limits of social development. Computers are only a tool for human beings. Centralisation and socialisation of knowledge and information is the necessity.

Some others found it inadequate and limited, and observed that knowledge could not and should not be restricted and centralised. The tendency to centralisation and centralism should be given up.

STR, Quantum Philosophy Modern Natural Sciences and Marxism

Anil Rajimwale's paper emphasised the urgent need to assimilate the conclusions of STR, modern natural and quantum mechanics and quantum philosophy so as to enrich Marxism. These developments have taken philosophy and theory to new levels. New philosophical problems are arising. Importance of dialectics has grown as never before. Hegelian dialectics has to be mastered, as did Marx and Lenin. Importance and role of motion and time has grown unprecedentedly.

Questions of subject-object relationships, relations between matter and idea, space, time, motion, etc. have taken on new dimensions. The newtonian world view is being replaced by the Einstenian world view. Many Newtonian laws are inoperable in the quantum world.

Quantum forces are becoming productive forces. Therefore, they have a growing social relevance. Computers, as also many others, are new productive forces.

Review Session: The Sum Up

All the participants warmly welcomed the initiative to hold the workshop, and suggested a number of continuation seminars-cum-workshops at all India and state levels. M. Vijaya Kumar, CR Foundation, NRRR Centre, and Anil Rajimwale were thanked for organising and pooling together their efforts.

More ground work and participation were desired. Dialectics, party education, post-modernism, virtual reality, etc. should be studied for their relevance. Discussions and conclusions of the workshop should be popularised and followed up. The party leadership should listen and pay attention to the discussions. They should try to learn. The conclusions of the seminar should be incorporated in the party documents. Theory should get greater importance.

The participants noted that there were no acrimonious exchanges; yet, there were very fruitful and educative debates, discussions and exchange of views of quite a high order.

Some participants noted that there were too many topics. Therefore, more pointed workshops should be organised in the coming period. The participants appreciated the advance circulation of the Base Discussion Papers and of the huge amount of reading material.

Contributors

1. **Anil Rajimwale:** General Secretary of All India Progressive Forum (AIPF), specialist in STR.
2. **M. Vijaya Kumar:** Working President, AIPF, scholar and scientist.
3. **Soma Marla:** A renowned geneticist.
4. **(Late) Y.V. Krishna Rao:** Specialist in agrarian questions and scholar on socialsim.
5. **Yugal J. Rayalu:** Political scientist, specializes in religious philosophy.
6. **Rameshwar Dass:** Historian and speacialist in future of socialism.
7. **Laxman Sigh Shekhawat:** A scientist-farmer, interested in the questions of socialism.
8. **C.R. Bakshi:** Well-known social activist and scholar on socialism.
9. **Krishna Jha:** Scholar on Soviet affairs, philosopher, researcher, and well-known journalist, specialist on gender question.
10. **Ishwar Singh Dost:** Researcher on democracy and socialism.
11. **Khagendra Thakur:** Intellectual and thinker on socialism, literary expert.

12. **Bhanudeb Dutt:** Specialist in the socialist movement.
13. **Ram Narsimha Rao:** Social activist and writer on socialism.
14. **H. Mahadevan:** A trade unionist and General Secretary of World Federation of Trade Unions (WFTU).